BENEATH THE BLAZING SUN

BENEATH THE BLAZING SUN

STORIES FROM THE AFRICAN-AMERICAN JOURNEY

REX M. ELLIS

August House Publishers, Inc.
LITTLE ROCK

Published 1997 by August House, Inc.,
P.O. Box 3223, Little Rock, Arkansas, 72203,
501-372-5450.

Printed in the United States of America
10 9 8 7 6 5 4 3 2 1
LIBRARY OF CONGRESS CATALOGING-IN-PUBLICATION DATA
Ellis, Rex M., 1951-
Beneath the Blazing Sun: stories from the African-American journey/
Rex M. Ellis.
p. cm.
Includes bibliographic references.
ISBN 0-87483-488-0 (alk. paper)
1. Ellis, Rex M., 1951- —Childhood and youth—Anecdotes.
2. Afro-Americans—Virginia—York County—Biography—Anecdotes.
3. York County (Va.)—Social life and customs Anecdotes. 4. Afro-Americans—
Folklore. 5. Afro-Americans—History—Anecdotes.
I. Title
F232.Y6E45   1997
975.5'42300496073--dc21   97-7086

President and publisher: Ted Parkhurst
Executive editor: Liz Parkhurst
Project editor: Suzi Parker
Assistant editor: Jan Cottingham
Editorial assistant: Chris McCarty
Cover design: Alex Cameron

AUGUST HOUSE, INC.   PUBLISHERS   LITTLE ROCK

To my mother, Margarett N. Ellis,
who has never lost faith in me.

And to Paulette, Amber, and Aaron

CONTENTS

INTRODUCTION

It was my first day of first grade in a school so big that it made me want to run back to kindergarten and do it all over again. The school was a huge, red brick maze that I constantly became lost in. But by Thanksgiving, I was so much at home that the janitor and I were on a first-name basis, and I knew so many new boys that we had to have three games of marbles going on, all at once, during recess.

From 1957 to 1964, I attended an all-black elementary school called Frederick Douglass in York County, Virginia. Everyone I knew went to that school. I had my first crush on a teacher at Douglass, my friend Carl Banks got hit in the head with a Coke bottle there, and that's where the boys played marbles during recess. That was the school where George Wallace, a boy who had repeated two grades, grabbed a black snake by the tail during recess one day, swirled him around counterclockwise, and then reversed the direction. The snap was so sharp the snake's head popped off! George was my hero until I left for high school.

All of my friends who lived in the same neighborhood also went to Frederick Douglass. Most of my teachers were from the area and went to my church or to one of the few other churches in that small community of East Williamsburg, Virginia.

I don't remember a great deal about the lessons I studied at Frederick Douglass. I remember learning my multiplication tables from Mrs. Montague. I probably remember that only because the day I didn't know my threes, she made me walk around the room saying I was a dummy while paddling myself. I remember my threes the best, even after all these years. I also remember English class, because we got to read out loud and write poems, which were always great fun.

But the best time of all was every Thursday, because that was the day we went to the library. Our librarian, Mrs. Rodgers, was the only white person in the school. That woman could tell a story! When she opened her mouth, you knew something important was going to come out. As she began to tell those stories from books she had selected from our library, my mind followed her to distant lands where imaginary people did incredible things. I ceased being myself in that library. I was battling an ogre, saving a young girl in trouble, or flying toward the stars. It was not until Mrs. Rodgers slowly closed the book that my mind returned to that green carpet we sat on and those oak tables and chairs that had been moved to the side in preparation for the imaginary journey. Who would have ever thought that I would be telling a story about Mrs. Rodgers?

As the years pass, I still clearly recall three vivid events from my elementary school years. First is the success I had in writing poems. One of my poems was even printed in a countywide collection of poems representing the best writing from local elementary schools. The second recollection is of President John F. Kennedy's inauguration. I remember watching it on the television that one of my teachers brought to school that day. It was so cold that you could see the breath coming from President Kennedy's mouth every time he spoke. Finally, I remember President Kennedy's assassination. I was in the seventh grade and we were acting up in class. When the teacher returned from the teachers' lounge to announce that President Kennedy had been shot, she asked us to be quiet. Then, when she returned a second time, she announced that the president was dead. She said, "Well, I guess you're satisfied. The president is dead!" For the longest time after that I thought he had died because we had shown such disrespect.

John F. Kennedy was the only white man I remember having such an impact on my neighborhood. Everyone was sad. Everyone acted as if a member of his own family had died. It took me awhile to understand that one. After all, the only white people my family knew were the people my mom cleaned house for and the ones my dad did brick work for. We learned very early in life that white people didn't think we were equal to them. They believed in segregation. They thought we were ignorant. We learned that the only way to combat this bigotry was to get an education. So, because we stayed as far away from whites as we could, and they did the same, race was not a major issue until we began going to school together.

In 1968, when I was in the eleventh grade, the black and white high schools in York County consolidated. I then went to York High, a predominately white school. Boy, did I feel like a duck out of water. For the first time in my life, I was going to school, riding the bus, sitting in class, eating lunch, and, worst of all, competing with white students daily. I came face to face with all of those things my parents ever said about white people. I began observing them to see if they really did hate black people, if they really did think that we shouldn't be going to school with them, and if they really did believe that we weren't as smart as they were.

I don't know of anyone from my neighborhood who did not believe that a proper education was the only real path to equality and respect in America. And everyone was always interested in how you were doing. If you made terrible grades, everyone knew about it and felt obliged to give you a lecture about what would happen if you didn't study hard and do well. They truly believed in that now-familiar African proverb, It takes a village to raise a child.

Although much emphasis was placed on the fact that learning should take place, I don't remember a great deal of conversation about what we were learning. I did not find myself questioning what I was learning until much later in my academic career.

You know, you don't really begin thinking about what you want to do with your life until it's almost time to graduate. Then the reality of entering the cold, cruel world stares you in the face. I didn't play first-string basketball, football, or baseball as many of my friends and classmates did, so there would be no sports scholarships for me.

Academically, I was a "B" student—no more, no less. My dad had completed the sixth grade, and my mom, the eighth. In my neighborhood, no one really expected me to do or be anything. Most folks thought I was a nice, sweet kid who would never go that far, because neither of my parents was brilliant. The genes told the story.

Then one day, someone recited a poem. I lit up like a Christmas tree. This was something I could do! Unlike all of those things I agonized over because I didn't do them well, here was something that came naturally. It was poetry. It was storytelling. It was as if Mrs. Rodgers were taking me to another place and time. But that day was extra special, because in my high school, anything sensitive and "girly" like reciting poetry labeled you a loser. No one thought it was cool. But on this particular day, Mr. Williams, the boxing champ of the whole school system, recited a poem. No one messed with Mr. Williams. If *he* was reciting a poem, I thought, then it must be OK for me to recite one, too.

When I began at York High, something else extraordinary happened. In my junior year, the school administration decided to produce the school's first musical, *Lil' Abner*. I auditioned and got the third lead. The only reason I didn't get the lead was because Lil' Abner was in love with Daisy Mae, and the teachers certainly couldn't have a black boy in love with a white girl, not in 1968 in Yorktown, Virginia. So I got the role of Marryin' Sam, and for me that was a turning point. I had found a niche.

The only problem was that everyone, especially my dad, was telling me that a career in theater was an irresponsible one. "Anybody can act like a clown," he'd say. This was not in his plans. He was looking forward to me becoming a doctor or lawyer.

But I had found something I did well and that I enjoyed. I performed every chance I got, and the more I did, the more I *wanted* to do it. I can't express how good it feels to have something that's yours, something that makes you feel as if you do have a purpose in life. I had to work on my dad for some time, until he attended my first performance. Then even he understood.

Everything that I have now accomplished has been a result of my foundation in the performing arts. I was too big for basketball, too small for football, and too slow for brain surgery, but I found *my way*. My way—not anyone else's. My voice. I discovered the contribution I could make in a way that motivated others to listen. But finding the source of my happiness began with Mrs. Rodgers on those Thursdays just before lunch.

✳ ✳ ✳

I was born in Claremont, a little town in Surry County, Virginia. When I was a year old, my family moved to Williamsburg, because my daddy thought he would be better able to find work on the other side of the river in Williamsburg. He was a brick mason, carpenter, plumber—he could do anything, it seemed.

For as long as I can remember, we lived on Queen's Creek

Road in a house that my father built single-handedly from the ground up. When someone asked where you were from in those early days, you generally replied "East Williamsburg," never "Queen's Creek Road" or "off Penniman Road," places that connoted a lower class neighborhood that most of my peers and I did not wish to associate ourselves with. In other words, it was too country.

So I grew up in the late fifties, sixties, and early seventies. Throughout those impressionable years, my family had only one television and that was a black and white Sylvania, I believe. The channel selector broke after many years, and we had to use a pair of pliers to change the channels. Back then television had only three networks—ABC, NBC, and CBS. I remember watching television shows like *Mighty Mouse, My Friend Flicka, Roy Rogers, Zorro, I Love Lucy,* and *Superman.*

Later in the sixties the shows were *Leave It to Beaver* and *Dennis the Menace,* and, when Mama wasn't watching, *The Twilight Zone.* Then there were *Bonanza, Gunsmoke,* and *Peyton Place.*

I was almost out of my teen years before I saw a commercial acknowledging that black people also sometimes had bad breath or body odor, and used Tide and Cheer to wash their clothes. We simply were not to be found on any commercials that talked about these things.

We were taught by television, radio, local newspapers, magazines, billboards, and the stores and shops we patronized that a beautiful woman was blonde, brunette, or redheaded. She had to have shaved legs, painted fingernails, wear makeup, tweeze her eyebrows, dress well, and have a fine figure. Handsome men were white and used Brylcreem in their hair. I can even remember when many black men tried to have "good" hair like whites by putting processes on their heads and buying instant status symbols like cars and clothes they couldn't afford.

Our only white heroes were Franklin and Eleanor Roosevelt and John F. Kennedy. Our black heroes were Lena Horne, Duke Ellington, Paul Robeson, Wilt Chamberlin, Bill Russell, Sammy Davis, Jr., Diahann Carroll, and a host of other entertainers and athletes who had "made" it. And, of course, Dr. Martin Luther King, Jr. I was an adult before I knew that civilization began on the continent of Africa and that Africans, our ancestors, had universities of learning that were attended by famous Greek scholars. I never knew that people like W. E. B. Du Bois, Charles H. Wesley, Carter G. Woodson, Luther P. Jackson, and John Hope Franklin were writing about black history before I was born, or that African scholars and leaders like Abuba-Kari I, Akmed Baba, and Askai Muhammad popular with European scholars before America was even a country. I didn't know about Granville Woods, Archie Alexander, Alain Locke, Ida B. Wells-Barnett, Maggie Walker, or any number of Africans and African Americans who were vacant from the history, math, science, and literature books we studied during my years in public schools.

This absence affected the way I viewed the world. More importantly, it affected how I felt about myself. Because I couldn't see myself in the things that surrounded me every day, I, like millions of black people, had to overcome my own negative thinking. At one point, I truly believed that African Americans were inferior. And this belief was supported by a decision made before I was born to exclude some pieces of my history and play up others.

✳ ✳ ✳

I grew up in a place that is the site of what many consider the world's foremost outdoor history museum—something many of my friends and I never understood or appreciated. Ironically, I never knew or even suspected that Colonial Williamsburg's significance had anything to do with me as an African American. To those of us who lived in the black community during the fifties and sixties, Colonial Williamsburg was simply a place to work. Like McDonald's, it was where we worked during the summer or after school to earn extra money. The significance of it as a place to visit was never even talked about, except by a few well-meaning teachers who were careful not to mention that it was the capital of a slave-holding colony. I remember once, during my years at Frederick Douglass, our class was marched to a nearby highway leading to the center of town to wave at Queen Elizabeth II, who was on her way to Williamsburg. I knew *she* was a special person, but it never dawned on me that she was coming to visit a famous place.

Almost everyone I knew worked there at one time or another. My brother worked as a dishwasher; my father once laid bricks at Bassett Hall, Mr. John D. Rockefeller, Jr.'s hangout; my uncle was a bellhop at the Williamsburg Lodge; and my next-door neighbor was the housekeeping supervisor for the Motor House. Full time, part time, after school, on weekends, during the summer, or following retirement, black people in town flocked to Colonial Williamsburg to pursue the almighty dollar. No one I knew was getting rich there, but no one was refusing the work either.

I once even worked as a busboy at the Motor House Cafeteria, now called the Woodlands. I left after about three weeks, frustrated by the low wages and tired of cleaning up after white folks.

Even then I sensed that there was something different about Colonial Williamsburg. It always had a special aura surrounding it. Whether you acknowledged it or not, it was there. It was as close as my best friend's father, who was a chef in one of the restaurants until his retirement. It was in the faces of all who worked there.

Whether you were a janitor, waiter, busboy, or maid, working at Colonial Williamsburg made you feel ashamed. The way people looked at you—a flippant gesture, a caustic glance, a condescending smile. Each took a toll no matter how subtle, no matter how small.

Each family handled that shame differently. My uncle rationalized it by bragging about the tips he made. Others asserted that their jobs were easy and they were just collecting a check. Still others mentioned fringe benefits like bringing home extra food given to them that would have otherwise been thrown out. My father simply refused to take us there to visit, and because he was a brick mason with a lot of jobs unconnected to Williamsburg, he could avoid working there.

I would be a full-time employee at Colonial Williamsburg before identifying the source of my dad's feelings. It was slavery. Colonial Williamsburg constantly reminded us all of a place and time that flourished because we had been slaves. That was why my dad and most black people who lived on the periphery of the town felt the way they did. They were forced by economics to work at a place that reminded them of a time they desperately were trying to forget, a time that was responsible for their continued dependence. No one maligned those who worked there. After all, Colonial Williamsburg was one of the area's largest employers. But anyone who went there to visit, I grew to learn, had to be white or crazy.

My knowledge of slavery and its legacy became equal to the rest of those living in my neighborhood. We understood what a slave was and knew only too well that we were not enjoying the rights of full citizenship—even I knew that—but that was all we knew. I didn't know any history about slavery and wasn't encouraged by anyone to learn it. Anything that brought up the institution responsible for our present condition was to be avoided like the plague. Grown-ups never talked about it, except to say how bad it was, and children never dared to bring it up.

So in addition to worrying about puberty, finding a girl-friend, acting cool, wondering what I was going to wear each day, doing homework, and dealing with hygiene problems, dating, and parents who didn't understand me, I had to deal with being black—and a black male at that. I didn't realize or understand the depth of racism in America, but I always knew, from the first time I was called a nigger, that I was different.

How do you tell stories about being black in America, and having to confront the pain and cruelty of prejudice, and make them useful? You certainly can't hide from it or ignore it, because it's all a part of who you are. My story is a legitimate part of American history in that it is a part of the language, the customs, the behavior, and expression of all of us—my particular experience notwithstanding. Just as it is, with no embellishments, codicils, or adaptations, my experience is a part of the American narrative as we find it, not as we believe it ought to be. B. A. Botkin says, "Folklore as we find it perpetuates human ignorance, perversity, and depravity along with human wisdom and goodness. Historically we cannot deny or condone this baser side of folklore...." It is a part of the narrative as well. As such these sometimes sorrowful stories should be preserved and told, not to perpetuate or follow their examples, but to illuminate and correct the flaws and evils they reveal.

Well, that's what I set out to do with my performing arts background. Throughout my years, I have tried to use my skills to tell and teach others about culture. I also have wanted not to just tell but also to help others realize how important we are to one another, that we sink or swim together. I have tried to suggest that there is more to African-American history than meets the eye. Storytelling has given me the forum to do just that. It has let me combine my interests in history, the performing arts, and education.

The stories in this book are a result of that coming together. They represent my growth and my attempt to grapple with being black in America. The stories begin where they should, in Africa, specifically West Africa, and continue in America. The stories are mine, but they are based on considerable research, reading, and many, many wondrous, frightening, and joyous moments of living. They are a testament to, and acknowledgement of, the great respect and admiration I have for my extended and nuclear family. Those are the people who taught me what I know and helped formulate the stories you will read.

None of the stories is meant to provide a history of the African or African-American experience. The stories are meant to be windows on certain perspectives that I have been particularly struck by as an African-American male living in the upper South during the last half of the twentieth century. The black experience is inextricably connected to the American experience. No single account, even in story form, can cover all that has happened and be faithful to the myriad turns and twists of our cultural record. These stories, songs, and poems, therefore, are meant to engender questions that compel the teller, as well as the listener, to explore, question, consider, and honor the tradition that these few samples represent. For they are only the tip of a continent, a people, and our common human experience. My hope is that these works serve as an introductory tool that motivates the reader to dig deeper into the broader issues and implications that they suggest.

Like Mrs. Rodgers, I have a chance to tell the stories in my own words. They will naturally have my voice. I don't apologize for my perspective. I am who I am because of how I was raised, the people I have met, my values and beliefs, and the choices I have made.

But I have a larger objective. If the only value to these stories lies in my experience, then I have failed. It is my hope that you will see something of yourself in these stories. I hope that you will also see something about all cultures and realize there is much to learn, much to appreciate, and much to celebrate.

Rex M. Ellis

AFRICAN ORIGINS

This chapter centers on African stories and traditions. The objective is to help the reader understand the circumstances that led to Africans arriving on the shores of North America.

The Europeans entered West Africa when the region was at its most vulnerable. Because the vast majority of West African societies could not defend themselves, and because the region had an abundance of natural resources—pepper, gold, ivory, grains, and human labor—Europeans saw the opportunities and exploited them.

After the colonies were established in the Americas, the need for labor to build communities and fashion economies grew rapidly. That need was met by the enslavement of Africans. Such large amounts of money were being made on the slave trade that Africans began to be referred to as black gold.

The slave trade, however, did not destroy African cultural traditions. Enslaved Africans brought their memories, knowledge, and customs with them to North America. This cultural legacy was embodied in their stories, music, and dance.

Storytellers were an integral part of the community. They served as historians, advisors to kings, praise singers, healers, diviners, and entertainers. The term *griot* became popular in West Africa long before slavery. It is related to the seventeenth-century French word *guiriot* and gained common usage in the empire of Ghana. These early *griots* began a tradition that convinced their listeners that they were truly the keepers of their community's cultural memory. It was through the *griots* that the stories in this chapter were passed down.

Africans did not arrive in North America devoid of culture, social sophistication, or civilization. On the contrary, they came with their own unique worldviews based on complex and sophisticated systems that, in many instances, rivaled those of their European captors. ✳

It Is Man

Many stories from African cultures, like those of other cultures, are meant to teach morals and values. In many West African communities, one of the worst crimes a person could commit was lying. African storytellers, known as *griots* in some cultures, not only told stories but were also musicians and historians. Great emphasis was put on the spoken word. The *griot* was an important person because he knew the genealogy of every member of his community and could recite it by heart. It was important that the *griot*, as historian, remembered the lineage correctly, for if a person could not prove ancestry, he could be relegated to the status of slave. Truth and honesty, therefore, were valued, and liars were scorned and ostracized.

This story shows the consequences to those who lie.

✳ ✳ ✳

*"It is man who imposes himself upon things,
and not things which impose themselves upon man."*

A hunter who was returning to his home after a long and unsuccessful day of hunting was walking through the woods. Suddenly he stopped short, certain that he heard a noise not too far from him. As he quieted himself and listened intently, he heard the music of a *kalimba* and a soft sweet voice singing:

"It is man who imposes himself upon things, and not things which impose themselves upon man."

Moving closer to the sound, he parted the leaves in a thicket, and there in a clearing sitting on a stump was a tortoise. She had a *kalimba* strung around her neck, and her head moved from side to side as she sang her enchanting song. Never before had the man heard such a wonderful sound! After listening to the tortoise for quite some time, he quietly stepped back on the path in the woods and headed for his home.

Each day the man returned to the spot where he'd first heard the tortoise, and each day he was transformed and filled with joy by the tortoise's singing and playing. One day he summoned up enough courage to approach the tortoise and ask her if he could take her home, where he might enjoy her music in comfort. The tortoise agreed with one stipulation: that he not reveal her secret to anyone. The hunter agreed and gently picked up the tortoise and took her to his home. For many days he kept his side of the bargain and did not reveal his secret to anyone.

One day a friend of the hunter's came to visit him, and because he was his best friend, the hunter told him about the tortoise. The friend promised he would keep the secret, but he was worried about the hunter, for no one had ever heard of a singing turtle. He lived in that house in the woods all alone and rarely saw any of the other people living in the nearby village. It was quite possible that the hunter had lost his mind. When the hunter's friend returned to the village, he told a friend of his about the hunter. And that friend told another and that one another, until after a day or two the story of the hunter and the tortoise reached the village chief. "Ha, ha, ha," laughed the chief. "A tortoise who can sing! Bring this hunter before me and let me hear his story. Ha, ha, ha." And so the hunter was brought before the chief with all of the villagers assembled to hear what the hunter had to say. "Is it true?"

asked the chief. "Do you have a tortoise that can sing?"

"Yes, I do," said the hunter. With that all of the villagers fell upon the ground doubled over with laughter.

"I do have a tortoise that can sing and I will prove it. Tomorrow morning I will bring my tortoise here and she will sing for you, and then we will see who has the last laugh!"

The chief replied, "And if you speak the truth, you may have as many of my possessions as you desire."

Happily the hunter returned home, and when it was bedtime, he slept and dreamed of riches and treasures. The next morning the hunter proudly walked before the entire village with his tortoise and her *kalimba*. Proudly he set her upon a stump and told her, "Play." The villagers were silent, and in hushed anticipation they listened for a sound from the tortoise. But the tortoise said and did nothing. She just withdrew her head and settled comfortably into her shell as tortoises customarily do. This time the hunter commanded in a loud voice, "Play!" That did not work, so he pleaded, "Play." Finally, on his knees, he begged, "Play, please play." But the tortoise did not make a sound.

As the sun sank in the West, the chief called for the executioner, and the hunter's head was severed from his body. At that moment the tortoise poked out her head, picked up the *kalimba*, and began to sing. The villagers were beside themselves with grief. "Our brother spoke the truth!" they cried. "He was telling us the truth!"

"Why did you sit by and let us do this thing?" asked the chief.

"I was happy in my little space in the woods," replied the tortoise. "The hunter fell in love with my music, and I loved him because he was able to hear the beauty of my music. One day when he came to hear me sing, he asked if he could take me home. I agreed but only on the condition that he not reveal my secret to anyone. He lied to me, and in my homeland a liar is worse than a thief."

With those words, the tortoise descended the stump and walked toward her home. As she continued walking out of sight, the villagers heard her singing:

> *"It is man who imposes himself upon things,*
> *and not things which impose themselves upon man."*

Musa and the Lesson of the Lion

Within the slave system, as it existed in Africa, slave own-ers had to constantly strike a balance between the enslaved person as worker and as human being. If enslaved people were not accord-ed some portion of human decency and respect, they would rebel in the only way they could. As a former slave once said, "Good masters had good slaves. Bad masters had slaves that they had bet-ter not turn their backs on."

* * *

Many, many years ago in Angola, there lived a king named Musa. And like all kings he was very, very wise. He treated all of his people with great respect, from the elders to the slaves. Well, he had a son who was old enough to know better but too young to care. One day Musa came upon his son abusing one of his slaves. "Crawl to me and kiss my hand!" commanded Musa's son. Immediately, Musa stepped in, scolded his son, and made him ask the slave for forgiveness, instead. To which Musa's son replied, "But Father, it was just a slave, only a lowly slave, and are not all slaves below us?" "Sit down," said Musa, "and I will tell you the lesson of the lion."

The story went: A lion was roaming through the forest one day when he came upon a dog. Now, as you know, most dogs are friendly animals and will do all they can to help others. Well, being very hungry the lion demanded food, and being very obedient the dog trotted into the forest to see what food he could find. After a time he succeeded in finding roots and berries and such things as he could find in the forest.

Then he returned to the lion and presented the food to him. The lion knocked the food from the dog's paw and growled, "I eat meat. Bring me meat or I'll eat you!" Once again the dog disappeared into the forest. After a time he succeeded in finding a hare, but before taking it to the lion he searched for some more berries. But these were special berries because they were poisonous. Carefully he stuffed the berries in the hare's gullet and then returned to the lion and presented it to him. The lion grabbed the hare and devoured it greedily. The dog waited ever so patiently until, finally, the lion fell dead.

"That was a disloyal dog," said Musa's son. "No," said Musa, "that was an unwise lion, because he learned too late that even a dog knows when it is being mistreated—even a dog."

I Was There

For enslaved Africans and African Americans, music was an important tradition and an integral part of every activity. From the moment work began in the fields to time allowed for recreation, music was a primary ingredient in slaves' unique ways of expressing their religious beliefs.

The banjo is not generally seen as having African origins, but it does. Dena Epstein in her book *Sinful Tunes and Spirituals* traces the banjo from the Gambia region of West Africa in 1621 through the Caribbean and into Maryland and Virginia as early as 1754. More recently, Cecelia Conway has provided us with a more comprehensive look at black banjo traditions. Her exhaustive study chronicles the connections between Africans, African Americans, and the banjo.

The banjo lost favor in the black community in the nineteenth century when it began to be defined as an instrument synonymous with slavery, secularism, and minstrelsy.

An attempt to rediscover the banjo and to acknowledge its importance in the history of African Americans was the motivation for this poem.

Before the Portuguese came
and staked their claim,
I was there.
Before barracoons were built
to house captured souls,
I was there.
In the heat of the night,
in the calm of the day,
when sloops and schooners stole them away,
when in coffles and chains they had nothing to say,
I was there.

When loneliness hurt
like a worrisome pain,
I was there.
When no one listened
and no one came,
I was there.
When darkness covered the shacks they called
home,
and "patterollers" watched them so they would not
roam,
and the air was filled with their melancholy groans,
I was there.

When day was done
and it was time for fun,
I was there.
When no work was demanded
'neath the blazing sun,
I was there.
When laughter was needed and it was time to dance,

and young folks strutted under the old folks'
glances,
and young girls finally gave young boys a chance,
I was there.

I was there in the good times.
I was there in the bad.
Didn't matter who played me,
just my sound made them glad.
A moment to pause, a moment to smile,
a moment to laugh if only for a while,
and I was there.

THE TRANSATLANTIC JOURNEY

The experience of enslaved Africans as they made the journey across the Atlantic Ocean to North America was one of great upheaval. Africans were forcibly taken to South America as well as the Caribbean, but this chapter focuses on those who came to North American shores. Perhaps the most difficult and terrifying period for Africans who made the trip from Africa to the New World colonies was the Middle Passage, the journey from West Africa to North America, South America, and the West Indies.

To acquire African slaves, European slave ship captains sailed to Africa with goods such as rum, brandy, cheap brassware, glass beads, textiles, old guns, cowrie shells (used as a form of currency in parts of Africa), and iron bars. African nations, particularly the Susus, Fulas, and others in the area of Sierra Leone, Guinea, and the Ivory Coast, traded their fellow Africans for these goods.

African men in good health were worth one hundred fifty gallons of rum each. African women were worth ninety-five gallons a piece. A slave captain's success or failure depended on his ability to get his human cargo on the ship and ready to leave as quickly as possible.

Throughout the seventeenth century, relatively small numbers of blacks lived in North America. It was not until the beginning of the eighteenth century that larger numbers of Africans were brought to the shores of America. During the three hundred and sixty years of the slave trade, it has been estimated that from the fifteenth century to the nineteenth century between twenty and fifty million Africans were uprooted from their homeland.

At first, blacks were treated as indentured servants and set free after five to seven years of servitude. But in time, Virginia, one of the largest slaveholding colonies, began establishing laws that made all Africans arriving on North American shores slaves for life. As larger numbers of blacks entered the colony, the laws restricting their movement became even more harsh and restrictive, completely relegating them to a life of oppression, cruelty, and servitude. ✳

They Told Me

At a women's convention in May 1851, Sojourner Truth, mother and former slave, talked about the trials she had endured in early America. Her reflections about her children were especially poignant. She said, "I have borne thirteen chilern, and seen 'em mos' all sold off to slavery, and when I cried out with my mother's grief, none but Jesus heard me!"

On board the slave ships, the rattling of chains, the lashing of whips, and the groans and cries of terrified and abused Africans were daily occurrences. Many tried to jump overboard, preferring death to the stench, squalor, and inhumane conditions on board the slave ships.

This story was written in honor of the many mothers who lost their children aboard slave ships that traveled from West Africa to the New World. These mothers experienced unique and terrible suffering.

❋ ❋ ❋

They told her she'd be all right. She and her baby. They told her she would not be harmed. The one thing that kept her going was that baby. They had seen one full season before the whites came to Elmina and stole them away. In the beginning the milk was strong with her, but then, after many days and nights of rancid food and meager rations, she dried up.

When the crew put them up on deck each day and she saw the brilliant sunlight, she realized how much she wanted life for her baby.

Each day one of the enslaved African warriors, the quiet one, made the others give way so she and the baby could have room to feel the breeze off the ocean and the tingle of the sun on their faces. She admired the sun. It respected no one, loved no one, and feared no one. It did not care about a slave ship and a mother with no milk for her only child. It was good and evil bound together in a ball of fire so bright that she could only briefly stare into its face.

The warrior held his tongue, but his eyes were like the vast plains of the Sahara, deep, flat, and lifeless at times, and then, at other times, burning with the fire of indignation. The spirit was strong with this one; even the devils left him alone. The crew members checked the warrior's chains each day because they did not want this one to get loose. His silence seemed to bother them, especially the ones who guarded him. It was as if his very silence hid some important secret they longed to know.

The only time the warrior came to life was when the crew brought the mother and her child on deck. He knew of their love of the sun, and he looked forward to their coming each day. Together they shared its power silently. Their ebony skin seemed to come alive under its sweltering blaze.

One day she saw his eyes look downward, to stare at the water. It was a long, lonely stare as if he longed to be with the sea. She understood that look. She had seen it many times since they'd left home. She had even seen some of the other Africans struggling to reach the ocean, but they were always beaten back. Only when they sat on their haunches and willed themselves to death did they finally get their wish to unite with the ocean mother. But the woman could not think of such things. She had to be strong for her child.

It was the child who kept the warrior alive, too. The mother was convinced of it, and in turn it was the warrior who kept them alive. When he saw them each day, he'd hold out his arms, and the baby would go to him as if he were her father. As she lay in his big arms, she cooed like a dove. She lay perfectly still as if all pain and suffering had ceased, and all the emptiness had somehow been filled. She seemed to be more alive and energetic when she saw him. Even though he did not speak, there was much said between them. His smile was a paragraph; his stare, a speech. His gentle touch created a shield that could not be penetrated by the most powerful guns their white captors had. He'd hold her in his arms, look toward the sun, and hum a strange and haunting tune. All was well on these occasions, if only for a while.

The others would have done anything for him. They would have fought their captors if he had just taken the lead and asked, but he was far away ... in his head. He was in there somewhere, and the only thing that brought him out was the baby named Mendiani. Sometimes he looked at her and then stared off into the waters. It was as if he were searching for the place from which he had come, but there was water all around and nowhere to go. Perhaps, the mother thought, he left a little Mendiani back there. Perhaps holding the baby gave him comfort beyond her understanding. There were times, when he first saw Mendiani, that he'd look as if he were going to break out into a big laugh, but something stopped him each time, and he'd just look down in the water.

Even with all the death and dying around, the mother wanted Mendiani to live. Then that fateful day came, and her life changed forever. Mendiani was so fretful and unhappy that day, and she had begun to cry. First a whimper, like a bird chirping, then louder, like the bark of a squirrel. The other women tried to help the mother calm the baby down. They hummed with her, they rocked with her, but they could not comfort her. Then one of the devils came over and said, "Shut that thing up or I'll throw her overboard." The mother pleaded with him to leave them be. She prayed that the calming spirits would come and soothe the child. She walked and rocked her, but Mendiani would not stop crying. The mother offered her dry breast, but the baby turned away. She asked for food, but they refused her.

All at once, the baby let out yet another yelp, and then it happened. The devil returned and grabbed the baby from the mother. Before she could think what to do next, the warrior came from nowhere and grabbed the devil by the arm. He was in so much pain from the warrior's grip that he screamed and dropped the baby. With the other hand the warrior caught Mendiani and gave her to the mother. A shot rang out and the warrior groaned in pain. Blood dripped down his leg, but even so he would not let the devil go. Such horror on one face and such hate on the other—no one had seen such before. Another shot rang out, but the warrior had turned the devil in the path of the gunshot and the bullet hit him instead. Others came to the guard's aid, but by now the other warriors stood up in defiant opposition and would not let them near the warrior or their fellow guard. Mendiani cried no more. Every eye was on the warrior as he held the devil tightly in his grip. No one spoke. It was as if they feared that by speaking they might incite the warriors further.

Then someone yelled, "Send for the captain!" As if that were a signal, the warrior looked around at the mother, then at Mendiani. For the first time, the mother saw him smile. With blood running down his legs, guns bearing down on him, and the weight of hateful stares from all the whites, he was smiling. Then he began to laugh. The warrior took the key that the devil had around his belt, unhooked his chain, and with the happiness of one who has just joined with the one he loves, he dragged himself to the railing and gave himself to the sea. They could see him waving and smiling as the waters held him afloat. Then, as if he had decided it was enough, he disappeared under the ocean with the silence they had all come to know.

After that day no one threatened them; no one mistreated them. She and Mendiani received food and drink before anyone else, but it was of no use. Mendiani would not eat, nor had she cried or spoken since the warrior died. The mother was worried. One day as the mother and her child were brought on deck, and more dead bodies were thrown overboard, Mendiani began to stare at the water. She stared the same way the warrior had before he took his life. "No! No! Noooooooo!" cried the mother. Quicker than the mother could have ever imagined, Mendiani threw herself over the railing. The mother screamed in horror and rushed after her child but the guards thinking she might jump too, held her fast. She called after Mendiani and promised her she'd make it all right, but her screams went unheeded.

The last she saw of her Mendiani, the child was smiling and waving, as if beckoning to her mother to join her. And then she was no more. The mother screamed as if her very life force were being ripped from her body and then fell limp. The guards continued to hold her fast, but by now they did not need to. Her body was there with them, but her spirit died that day. She walked and she ate, she watched and she waited, but she died that day. The only thing that kept her going was a promise she made to herself that she would kill them all before the ship landed.

But she didn't. She continued to breathe even in the new land called Virginia. She had many children in this new land of America but none as precious as the one called Mendiani.

Olaudah Equiano

Olaudah Equiano, also known as Gustavus Vassa, was one of the few Africans who left a written record of his captivity and subsequent enslavement during the colonial period. From enslavement in Africa to his eventual freedom from his master in England and return home after many years and countless adventures, his story is one worthy of telling and retelling. Not only does the account of his life afford the reader a provocative and dramatic story, it also offers a great deal of information about West African culture.

Equiano's narrative was incredibly popular and more widely read than any other work by a black writer prior to 1789. Many historians also note that his ability to move from an oral culture to a literary one was an extraordinary accomplishment.

An Igbo prince from the area of Africa now known as Eastern Nigeria, Equiano was born in 1745 in a province known as Essaka. When he was eleven years old, Equiano was kidnapped and sold into slavery. How he and his sister were captured, and the circumstances that began his amazing journey, is the substance of this story.

* * *

Prince Equiano had just finished throwing his javelin, an activity that all young warriors were expected to participate in. He prided himself on the skill he had already begun to display. But after a full half day of this sport, he decided to find some of his friends and play. This was the way of their lives in his community. When the adults went out to work the fields, the younger children gathered to play and get into as much mischief as they could before their parents returned from the field and discovered their devilment. As they played, some of the older boys would climb the tallest tree and look out for the kidnappers who often came to steal them away. These African rogues knew that if their parents were away, they had a better chance at successfully carrying off helpless children. But most of the time the children were safe. As long as they stayed within the walls of the village, they had little to fear.

One day Equiano and his sister were left to mind the house as his family went off to the fields to work. Two men and a woman climbed over the wall and kidnapped them. The kidnappers put their hands over the children's mouths so their screams would not be heard and quickly carried them off into the woods. They carried Equiano and his sister toward the coast with their mouths gagged. They stopped at a house after a while and stayed the night.

The next morning, they started out, and for most of the day they traveled through the woods. Finally they came to a road where Equiano saw people walking in the distance. He called out to them, but his captors stopped his mouth and rushed him and his sister into the nearby woods. They put him in a sack, and there he remained for the rest of that day. At the end of the day, they stopped again. This time he and his sister were offered food, but they refused to eat.

The next day he and his sister were separated. They pleaded with their kidnappers not to separate them. They promised to be good and that they would not try to run away, but their pleas went unheeded. His sister was taken away. For a long time, Equiano grieved her loss. She was the only part of his life that gave him comfort. While she was with him, he at least had someone who was part of the life he had known. But now she would not be around so they could comfort each other in their confusion and misery. He refused to eat the food the captors offered him, but they forced it into his mouth.

After several days he was then given to a new master. This one was a chieftain and a blacksmith. He put Equiano to work on the bellows, stoking the fire. He worked for this man about a month. ·

Finally, seven months after he had been captured, Equiano arrived on the coast of the Atlantic Ocean. As he was marched toward the coast, he saw land that was very rich, and pomkins, plaintains, and yams were plentiful. Everywhere he went he saw tobacco and cotton growing wild.

Then he finally saw the two things that would be a part of his life for many years to come, a slave ship and the ocean. Never before had he seen so much water and so large a vessel. He was pushed on board the ship and then tossed about to see if he was healthy. The men who examined him were not like any he had ever seen. Their skin was white and they had long hair. The language they spoke was like none he had ever heard. He looked around the ship and saw black people of every description chained together. They all looked like he had felt the day his sister was taken from him. He was so horrified by what he saw that he fainted on the spot.

When he awoke, people were all around him. Some of them tried to cheer him up, but it didn't help. He asked them if the white men with ugly faces were going to eat him. They told him no. Then they gave him a drink of whiskey to calm him. He was so repulsed by the taste of it that he felt as if he were going to die. They then put him below deck. The slavers packed so many Africans below deck that many of them died from the heat and the inhuman conditions of that small place. The smell was so rancid and rotten that

Equiano became sick to his stomach. Two white men offered him food but he refused it. For this they tied him to a board and whipped him. The pain was greater than anything he had ever experienced. He had never been treated in such a way. He told himself that if the chance came, he would jump overboard. Death was preferable to this kind of treatment.

After a time he saw men on the ship who were a part of his nation. They told him that they were all going to be carried to the white man's country to work for them. This eased him somewhat, but these strange white men, who were so cruel, still frightened him. Surely working for them would only bring more hardship. They were even cruel to each other. One day Equiano saw one of their own kind flogged with a rope so badly that he died from it. They tossed him overboard as if he were nothing more than an animal. At every turn he saw them do horrible things that none of his countrymen would ever attempt. One day, when they had captured a large number of fish, they proceeded to kill as many as they planned to eat, and instead of giving the leftovers to Equiano and his countrymen, they threw the fish overboard. This was done while the Africans pleaded for the leftovers. Some of his countrymen were so hungry they tried to sneak food when the whites were not looking. Each one caught was severely flogged. One day he saw three of his enslaved comrades escape the safety netting and dive into the sea. Two of them drowned, but the third was captured. He was flogged. It seemed to Equiano that hardship, misery, and death would be his constant companions, and that the evils of the slave trade would be a part of his life for some time to come. He lay his head down each night in the cramped area below deck hoping that fortune would smile on him and let him see his sister just once more.

STRANGELY AMERICAN

How did Africans learn to survive in America? With no initial understanding of the language, customs, or mores of their captors, how did they form new values and beliefs? How did they live as slaves and still continue to hope for freedom, to live in fear but not allow fear to destroy their humanity?

During the eighteenth century, when America began forming a personality and culture all its own, new patterns of behavior and even friendships between cultures emerged. Because Africans and Europeans worked side by side, lived close to one another, and were dependent on each other, they came to borrow, learn, and adopt many characteristics common to each other's cultures. Those connections and associations continued until cultural lines began to blur. The blurring eventually created a new cultural worldview.

During the colonial period, enslaved blacks cooked, cleaned, planted, reared their own children, as well as the masters' and mistresses', and served as confidants, confessors, and trusted soul mates in countless households. The relationships that developed were complex. They varied according to age, sex, type of work done, and the proximity blacks had to their owners and their families.

Freedom was precarious in colonial America. Free blacks were better off than those enslaved, but their lives were also difficult. Although they could move to northern and western areas where there were no other enslaved Africans, no place they went was slavery illegal. In addition, a white person could claim ownership of a slave and win custody of him or her with no proof needed other than his word. Blacks could not testify against whites, so they had little recourse unless they could find a friendly white to testify on their behalf.

There were several ways a black could be free. For most of the eighteenth century, all free black women's children were free at birth. A slave could buy his or her freedom or receive it in a will or a deed of manumission.

Despite the strictures forced on the free black community, freedom was certainly preferred over a life of servitude, and blacks sought to emancipate themselves any way they could. ✳

Jack and the Fish

Many stories from the black experience focus on superstition—skulls talking, snakes crawling, and the dead walking. Many stories also teach customs, beliefs, and values. During the Great Awakening, a sweeping movement in the eighteenth century to popularize the Christian religion, many blacks embraced Christianity and became Methodists, Presbyterians, and Baptists. Sunday was important not only as a day of worship but also because it was the one day of the week most slaves were free from work. Although some families saw Sunday as a day of worship and rest, many saw it as a day to have fun. Many blacks living in colonial America enjoyed fishing on Sundays. The following story is one that could have been used by a mother wishing to convince her son that fishing on the Lord's day was bad luck.

* * *

In the town of Williamsburg, Virginia, there once lived a young boy named Jack. In those days, black people were slaves and most slaves did not have last names. Black people usually got one day off a week and that day was Sunday. That was the day that Jack would go fishing. He loved to fish. It didn't matter if he caught anything or not; he just loved to fish. He'd get his seine and weir nets, or he'd just use his pole, and he would go down to Queen's Creek, which was not far from where he lived, and he'd sit on his favorite side of the creek and fish.

Well, Jack's mother had recently become a Christian, and one thing she was strict about was behavior on Sundays. Sunday was a day of rest, and you were supposed to rest. No working, no fishing, no nothing. So Jack's mother warned, "Jack, I don't want you to go down to that creek anymore on Sundays because that's a day of rest."

Jack said, "Mama, I love to fish. I fish every Sunday and I'm gonna fish this Sunday too."

She cautioned, "Jack, I'm mighty afraid something is gonna happen to you. If you go fishing on Sunday, it means we are disrespectin' the Lord. Something bad might happen to you."

Jack said, "Can't be nothin' worse than being a slave. I'm going fishin'!"

Well, Sunday came and, just as he had said, Jack prepared himself to go fishing. He went to the fireplace and removed a piece of cornbread his mother had just baked in the dutch oven. He put the bread in a sack over his shoulder. He went out into the tobacco field and picked some nice, fat tobacco worms off some of the leaves, collected his fishing gear, and started out. Pretty soon he arrived at Queen's Creek. He walked to his favorite spot, sat down, baited his hook, threw his line in the water, and waited.

He figured it would take some time before the fish began to bite, so he reached for his piece of cornbread. As he was about to take a taste of it, he felt a tug on his line. Well, Jack started pulling back on that line, and he noticed that the line was hard to pull. He put down his cornbread and pulled with both hands. But no matter how hard he pulled, he could not pull that line back. He pulled with all of his strength but could not move that line. All of a sudden the line started pulling him. Jack tried his best to pull back on the line, but the line continued to pull him toward the edge of the water. Jack decided that he did not want to see whatever was on the other end of the line. He dropped his pole and started running toward home. Before he could go five steps a haunting voice came out of the water and said, "Stohhhppp!" Jack wanted to keep running but he had to stop.

The voice said, "Tuuuuurrrn Arooooouuuund."

Jack slowly turned around, even though he was trying not to with all his might. The voice commanded, "Raaaaaaisssse your hands!" Jack wanted to keep his hands still, but he could not control them. He raised his hands. It was as if they had a life of their own.

The voice said, "Drop your hands!"

Jack tried to resist but he had to drop his hands.

Then the voice ordered, "Waaaaalk." Jack wanted to scream, but he couldn't. He wanted to cry, but he couldn't. He wanted to run home to his mother, but he was under the power of the voice. He found himself walking toward the water, to the place from which the voice was coming. But he kept his eyes closed tightly so that he would not see whatever it was.

When he reached the edge of the water the voice said, "Stohhhppp." Jack stopped. The voice said, "Ohhhppen your eyes." Jack tried with all his might to keep his eyes closed, but it was no use.

Aaaaaaaagh! What he saw almost made him faint! The creature's left leg was made of seaweed, and sticks and bugs poked out from the leg. The other leg, made of mud, oozed with blood. Its chest resembled fish scales, and snake heads slithered out of it with their tongues flailing and their fangs showing. When the creature smiled, maggots and worms poured out of its mouth. But the worst part was its eyes. They burned red like the devil's. Then the creature said, "Look dowwwwnnn." Jack looked down and ... and ... and ... *his* left leg turned into seaweed. *His* right leg turned into mud and started bleeding. Snakeheads slithered out of *his* chest, bugs poured out of *his* mouth, and *his* eyes burned red! The voice said, "Look uuuuuup." Jack looked up and the creature had turned into Jack! The creature said, "Since you love to fish, you live with them ... and I'll live with men."

Jack has not been heard of from that day to this. You know, nobody goes down to Queen's Creek anymore to fish. And *nobody* goes down there on Sundays.

The Wolf and the Dog

During the colonial period, most Africans and African Americans were enslaved. A comparatively small number were free. They either had bought freedom from their masters, or they had fought in a war and received freedom in exchange for their service. That number, however, was small, and during this oppressive and dehumanizing time, some blacks ran away whenever they could, while others stayed, believing they were valued members of their owners' extended families.

The following story addresses this phenomenon using the character of a wolf, who, like many blacks of the period, chose to live a life of freedom, a life of running away and hiding out—with little comfort—and the dog, who embraced a life of comfort—albeit accompanied by humiliation, degradation, and contempt.

✻ ✻ ✻

Once there lived a dog in Williamsburg, southeast Virginia, and he had a friend, Wolf, who lived in Charlottesville, north-central Virginia. Every so often they'd visit one another. Well, this particular weekend, Dog decided he would visit Wolf. When he arrived at Wolf's home, he felt like bragging. So he said to Wolf, "You know, you know, my master loves me. He treats me good. I eat roastin' ears and ham and chicken. When it rains outside, I'm nice and dry inside. When it snows outside, I'm nice and warm inside my master's house. Look at you! You're livin' in a hollow log. When it rains, it rains on you. When it snows, you nearly freeze to death. You're eatin' roots and berries and bugs and moths. I can even see your ribs. You look pitiful, just pitiful!"

Wolf said, "Yeah, that's right. But since your master loves you so much, I'll tell you what. When you go home tonight, why don't you ask your master if I can come down there to Williamsburg and live with you, since he loves you so much!"

Dog said, "All right ... all right ... all right, because he loves me."

So Dog went back down to Williamsburg. But Wolf didn't trust Dog, so he followed him. When Dog got to the house of his master, he began to scratch on the door and whine, "Muh, muh, muh, muh, muh, muh." But the master couldn't hear, so Dog hollered, "Roor, roor, roor, roor!"

The master opened the door, saw Dog, grabbed him by the collar, and yanked him inside the house. Wolf was curious now, so he sneaked up to a window and peeked inside. He spotted a table full of food and a chair beside it. The master was sitting in the chair, and Dog was in front of him, clowning and dancing in a ridiculous way, "Roor, roor, roor, roor." That tickled the master, so he threw Dog a chicken leg. Dog caught it in one gulp. "Roor, roor, roor!" Dog intensified his antics. That tickled the master and he threw him a piece of ham. "Roor, roor, roor." Dog chased his tail and jumped up and down.

About this time the master grew tired of Dog's buffoonery, so he put his head on the table to sleep. Well, Dog was still hungry, so he began to whine again, "Muh, muh, muh." But the master couldn't hear this because by now he was fast asleep. Dog took those doggy claws and dug them into the master's knee. "Roof!" Dog bellowed. The master jumped up and saw it was Dog. He kicked Dog to the door, opened the door, and threw Dog out of the house. Dog rolled to Wolf's feet.

Wolf said, "Yeah, your master loves you, huh? I may not know where my next meal is coming from, and I may not live in a fine house, but nobody treats me like they treat you. You stay here in Williamsburg. I'm going on back to Charlottesville." And that's exactly what he did.

IN THE FACE OF FEAR

The stories in this chapter are dedicated to the men and women throughout history who have resisted oppression and actively fought for the betterment of the African-American community. Each was willing to love themselves and their people enough to face untold danger in hopes that they might make it better for themselves and others.

African Americans understood that to have a better life they had to take chances. They had to look in the face of danger and make sacrifices. Those who took chances and stared danger in the face became heroes. Some of these heroes include people such as Venture Smith, Denmark Vesey, Nat Turner, Harriet Tubman, and Sojourner Truth. Others include mythical characters such as John Henry, High John the Conqueror, Dolomite, and Big John.

African Americans have historically glorified tough characters with "grit in their craw." These are the men and women who have had the courage or, as some might say, the foolhardiness to rush in where angels fear to tread, daring to stand alone. The only opportunity that many of these people had to develop was in the world of work or the fields of labor or during the few times when they were allowed to entertain themselves at parties that bred the bad men and women who became heroes of their people.

Although heroes are much more colorful than the rest of us, something special exists about the average working man. He suffers through the drab existence of everyday life, yet sometimes achieves extraordinary fame and success by simply doing the best he can with what he has. ✸

Big John and Slick Sam

Many African-American heroes were inspired by the thousands of enslaved Africans, men and women, who resisted the system of slavery in one way or another. Perhaps all they did was break a hoe, pretend to be sick, or work as slowly as possible, but they still defied the odds and tried to rebel against the slave masters who oppressed them and denied them the right to determine their own future. It is no accident that many of these characters had some edge or advantage. Some were physically powerful; others were skilled as blacksmiths, tanners, tailors, musicians, and carpenters and used their talents to gain an advantage over oppression. Some like Solomon Northup, Simon Gilliat, and London Brigs used their gifts as musicians. Others used their "divine calling," becoming ministers of the gospel. With many, wit and intelligence won the day. Such was the case with Slick Sam.

* * *

Two slave owners were relaxing on a porch one day bragging about their slave men. "I've got the strongest and meanest slave that ever walked the face of the earth over at my place, don't ya' know," said Hank Green.

Green was a pretty good man, especially for a white man who owned slaves. He was probably more decent than most. He gave his slaves Sunday off from working, and he made sure that all who wanted baptism received it. He gave them most holidays off, and when they got sick, he tried to give them the best doctoring in the county.

But there was one he treated even more special, and that was the strongest, meanest, and hardest worker he had—Big John! "What's so great about this Big John?" asked Green's neighbor and friend, Jim Connor.

Connor and Green had been friends for years. They met at least twice a month to see who could tell the biggest lies and spit tobacco the farthest. They spent most of their time on the front porch, drinking lemonade and eating ginger cookies, which Green's wife always made when Connor visited because she knew they were his favorite. Like good neighbors, they helped each other out. If Green was going into town to get supplies, he'd stop and ask Connor if he wanted to send for something. If Connor was headed to town, he'd return the courtesy.

But they also loved to argue. Any subject would do—the weather, how many acres they could tend in a day, which one of their wives was the best cook. Why, they even argued about how far each of them could spit! No subject existed that didn't have the potential for stirring up a good argument.

But on this day, they started arguing about something that would lead them to a subject they usually avoided. They began an argument about their slaves—in particular, which one of their slaves was the best. Both men loved to gamble, and if one of their arguments led to a friendly bet, then all the better. Lots of slave owners gambled, so why couldn't they?

"Well," Green said, "last week, we were finishing the hay harvest over near the north quarter. One of my wagons was loaded to the tiptop with bales of hay, and my people had hitched up my ox, ol' Juba, to the wagon. All of a sudden, without any warning, Juba let out a groan so loud you could hear it a mile away. Then all of a sudden he just dropped to the ground. *Wham!* I'd swear the ground shook when he hit.

"The foreman rushed over to him, took one look, and knew what had happened. He had broke his leg. It was bent back in a way that God had not intended for man or beast, and poor Juba was groaning and trying to get up at the same time.

"Some of the women came over and tried to comfort the poor thing. He'd stepped into a sinkhole while carrying that load, and the force of the twist just snapped his left shank like a dried twig, don't ya' know.

"One of the old African men who was good with roots told the foreman that if he could just get the ox back to his stall in the barn, maybe he could leave the wagon where it was until daybreak. They thought about unloading the wagon and putting that ol' ox in it. But Juba weighed eight hundred pounds when he was just a baby. There was no way they were going to get that great big ox in that wagon.

" 'Well, we got to try something,' someone said.

"So they grunted and strained, and strained and grunted, and grunted and strained, but ten of the strongest men I had couldn't get that ox to budge from that spot, don't ya' know.

"Then somebody hollered, 'Go get Big John! If he can't move Juba, nobody can!' So Jessee's boy Harvey ran off to get John.

"Big John was still in the back field throwing hay bales on a second wagon, so one of the young 'uns went to git him so's he could help. After a while, you could hear the ground shakin' underneath your feet, and the wagon with the hay in it was rumblin' like it was an earthquake comin'. You couldn't see John yet, because as his big feet hit the ground, he kicked up so much dirt that he was lost in the cloud of dust that he made as he ran. It was like a small tornado coming across the field.

"As John got closer you could see him plainly, and poor little Harvey was covered with dust as he trailed behind Big John, coughing and sneezing!

"John is bigger than two men, and you could see him growing bigger and bigger the closer he got. The ground rumbled and shook even more. Some of the slaves had to hold onto each other to steady their feet as the ground quaked under them.

"When John got to the place in the field where everyone else was, he asked in that big, booming voice of his, 'What's wrong wit' Juba?' They told him what had happened and that they needed to get Juba to the barn but that they couldn't pick the ox up to put him on the wagon.

"John said, 'Step aside.' He walked over to that ox, put one arm under his middle close to his front legs, the other arm under his middle close to his rear and picked that ox up! Didn't even put him in the wagon. He carried Juba back to that barn and laid him in that stall just as gently as you would a newborn baby, don't ya' know! Ten men couldn't move ol' Juba, but John picked him up like he was a puppy dog."

"That's the biggest lie ever been told," Connor said. "You made that up just as sure as my toenails are long! I never seen nobody who could pick up a full-grown ox. You are a bigger liar than the man down at the fair who tells all them tall tales about headless men walking around.

"Besides," he continued, "strength ain't everything. Roughest slaves I own ain't the strongest ones; they's the smart ones. I got a man by the name of Sam that can outwrestle, outfight, and outsmart any man in the county, black or white."

"What makes you think he's such a good wrestler?" asked Green.

"Last winter, we went up to Charlottesville to do some bear huntin'. The second morning we were there, we spotted a black bear. I had seen bigger, but he was still about three hundred pounds, I figured. He was no more than ten yards away, so I raised up my gun to shoot at him.

"At that moment, I heard a growl behind me. It was the mama bear, and she was so close to me I could see the snot streaming out of her nose!

"I started to run and she started after me. I ran to the nearest tree, grabbed a strong branch, and pulled myself up just before she swiped at me with them razor-sharp claws. But once I got up that tree, I noticed something that scared me even more. I had left my gun on the ground right in front of that bear, and he had stepped on it and broke it half in two. I had dropped the only gun we had on the ground, and there it lay with a broken stock, useless.

"I yelled for Sam to run away, but instead of running, he reached in his belt and pulled out that old hunting knife I let him wear when we are out in the woods, and he started after that mama bear. As he ran toward her, she turned and started headin' for him.

"Just then, Sam got this strange look in his eyes and let out a scream that was the most frightening sound I've ever heard. That bear stopped in her tracks. Then I noticed Sam wasn't going for the mama bear. He was going for the baby that was watching all of us up on a hill, just over a rise! Sam screamed again and that little bear was so scared he turned to run. The mama took off after them both, but she couldn't catch Sam. He ran into the brush and on out of my sight. I heard him scream that horrible scream of his once more, and the bear let out a growl of her own.

"After that it was silence. When I thought it was safe, I got down out of the tree. At that moment, I heard a bloodcurdling growl from the bear off in a distance and then silence again. Now I was gettin' real scared. I didn't know whether to run for the cabin or run for Sam.

"I picked up a big stick and started walking in the direction where Sam had gone. As I got closer toward the spot where Sam had run, I saw him walking toward me. Sam had the mama bear's head in his hand and this big grin across his face.

" 'We gon' have steaks and sausage and all kinds of meat come winter, Master! He was holding the bear's head by its ears. He had cut it off as clean as you'd shave the hairs off your face!

"That was sure some tasty bear meat. I gave most of it to the slaves, though. Sam said, 'Give it to them. I can always git more!' "

· "Now that lie is so big you should git a prize, don't ya' know," complained Green.

"Come on over to my house, and I'll show you the bear's head," said Connor. "I had it stuffed for doubting Thomases just like you. That Sam is a pistol and that's a fact!"

"Looks like your man and my man is gon' have to meet up," said Green.

"Looks like it," agreed Connor. "And to sweeten it up a bit, I'll bet you a wagonload of white potatoes that my man Sam can kick your man John up and down these hills—or have him so scared he'll run for cover to keep from fightin' him."

"Let's make it two wagonloads. That's my whole crop this year, and that's how sure I am that my John will knock your Sam in the tall corn."

"It's a deal," said Connor. "I'll meet you at the old Howard place with my people next Saturday, and we'll see who is who and what is what!"

Connor returned to his house to tell Sam that he had arranged a fight and that he had to fight Big John over at the old Howard place.

Sam said, "I don't know iffen I can beat John. He's the strongest man I ever seen. They still talking 'bout how he picked up that ox and totted him to the barn the other week. Said he wasn't even winded when he got to the barn."

"Well," said Connor, "I heard about it too, but I don't believe everything I hear. And even iffen he did what they say, there's more than one way to win a fight. I told Hank you would either beat his boy or scare him so bad that he would run away from you, and if you wants to keep them three children you got with you, you'd better not make me out to be a liar! I bet him all of our white potatoes that you'd win. If you lose, you won't ever see them children again, 'cause I'll sell every one of them off. You hear me?"

"I'll think of something, Master," said Sam. As he walked away toward his cabin, he mumbled to himself, "I can't lose my chillen. I just can't lose my babies."

On the day before the fight, Sam took a shovel and a hoe and went over to the old Howard place. A tall oak tree stood near the flattened area where the fights in the county usually took place. Sam began to dig the dirt from around the roots of that big oak tree. All day long he dug, exposing root after root until that tree was just about ready to topple over. After he had loosened the dirt, he put fresh dirt back around the tree and packed it loosely. Then he spread leaves and acorns and brush around it so that it looked as natural as any other tree in the area. Then he swept out his tracks with a broom made of brush until he was satisfied that he had left no trace of what he had done. "That ought to do it," he said to himself as he started for home.

The next morning, Connor went out to the quarters to get Sam. When he walked into the quarter, he was amazed to find that Sam was tied up with a vine just like the ones found growing in the woods out back of his quarter. He'd had his wife tie him up. But what Connor didn't see was that Sam had his wife cut into the strongest part of the vine, near the middle of his chest, just enough so that he could break loose from it just by tensing his muscles.

Sam turned to his wife and whispered, "Don't you worry, honey pot. We gonna be eatin' taters until the cows come home."

When Connor asked Sam about the vine, Sam explained, "I figured I'd seem like I was meaner iffen everybody thinks I'm so wild that you got to tie me up to keep me in line."

"Good thinkin'," said Conner as he picked up one end of the vine and started leading Sam out of the quarter.

"Wait," said Sam. "I got to put my crazy face on." Right before his eyes, Connor saw Sam work himself up to a point where he thought the man had lost his mind. He was growling and wheezing and howling and spitting like a wild man. All of a sudden he stopped, winked at Connor, and nodded his head, signaling that he was ready to walk out to meet his fans.

As Connor and Sam walked out of the quarter, the other slaves who lived on lands that Connor owned had already gathered. They all wanted to witness this fight. It had been the talk of the county, and Big John was the heavy favorite. Some of Connor's slaves even bet on Big John. The majority were betting on Sam, but even they had their doubts.

"If he wins this one, it'll be a miracle!" exclaimed one.

"I just hope John don't beat him too bad," said another.

"Shush now. Here they come."

They all followed behind Sam and wished him good luck. Even with all of his growling and howling, they didn't think he had much of a chance. Figuring Sam would need all the help he could get, a few of them even knelt down for a word of prayer.

When they arrived at the Howard place, there were so many people that they could hardly hear Sam growling. Then someone yelled, "There he is! There he is! There's Sam! Looks like he's ready to fight too!" It looked as if the whole county were there.

As Connor walked Sam in, Big John was sitting on a stump relaxing himself. He looked like the cat who had swallowed the canary. He was so haughty and sure of himself that he was bragging to a group of teenage boys about what he was going to do to Sam and how he was going to knock him into the sweet peas.

"When I finish with him, his wife won't know who he is," Big John said. "They'll have to change his name to Lumpy, 'cause he's gon' have plenty of bumps on his big head. Haw, haw, haw!"

As Big John continued boasting, he looked up and saw between two of the boys what appeared to be Sam approaching.

"Move out of my way, boys," demanded Big John. "I don't believe what I'm seeing." Now John could clearly see Sam being led in by a vine wrapped around him.

John turned to his master and asked, "Why he got to be tied up like that?"

Connor heard him as he and Sam arrived on the spot and explained, "I got to keep him tied up, or else he'll jump loose and attack the first person he sees. When I went to get him this morning, he was eating onions and growling like a madman. I think he's been talkin' to them ghosts again."

"What ghosts?" asked Big John, who was deathly afraid of anything from the other world.

"Oh, it's nothing I believe in, but Sam claims that when he talks to his ghosts, they give him the strength of fifty men."

"Don't listen to these lies, John," said Green. "They's just trying to scare you."

Connor tied Sam to the big oak tree and made sure the vine was nice and tight. Then he stepped back out of the way.

All of a sudden Sam's eyes started rolling around in his head, he started foaming at the mouth, and he began to shake as if he were possessed. He let out a yell that shook the entire gathering. Little children clung to their mamas, youngsters who could run were backing up fast, and old people, who knew it would take them longer to get away, reached for their canes and crutches.

Sam let out a bone-chilling scream and hollered, "They's here! My ghosts, they's here!" He looked down at the ground and began to call for the devil. "Come to me, Prince of Darkness; come to me, monster of the deep; come to me and help me beat my enemies up here in this place!" Then he let out an eerie laugh and began to strain and grunt and groan.

Everybody in the crowd stood up and started to move back fast. Big John said, "Master, look at him! He's possessed! Lord have mercy, he's possessed!"

Sam yelled, "I'm coming for you ... I'm coming for you all ... but I'm gon' get you first, Big John. Yeeeee haaaaaaa!!!"

He grunted one last time, and the tree he was tied to began to pull away from its roots. As it did, Sam moved forward and the tree looked as if it were going to fall on Big John. All of a sudden the vine snapped in two and Sam lunged at Big John.

"I got it! I got the powerrrrr!" cried Sam.

All of the slaves jumped back in horror. Big John turned and began to run. Green was right behind Big John. Everywhere people were running for their lives. Old people hobbled and shuffled. Young people were running into trees, stepping on each other as they tried to get away. Even the dogs and horses headed for the hills!

But in front of them all was Big John. His eyes were as big as silver dollars, and he was so scared that he stepped on people as he ran. It was as if he had a fire in his behind. They say that Sam ran him so far that he kept on running until he reached the county line.

Sam and his family ate fresh pork and white potatoes all winter, and from that day on he was known as Crazy Sam, the best man in the county.

Amos the Snake

Like many people, I have always been afraid of snakes. My scariest dreams as a child always focused on snakes. Then one day I was confronted by a snake and I killed it. My sudden reaction to the snake surprised me, and for a while I felt triumphant. Then as I took a good look at the dead snake, it occurred to me that maybe the real problem was not the snake but my own prejudice against the snake. I had listened all of my life to what everyone I loved had said about snakes, and I allowed their beliefs to become mine. I prejudged snakes and assumed they were my natural enemy and, therefore, creatures to fear.

But what if there were some way for me to get to know a snake? Would I still be afraid of it? Would I still think it was my enemy? Would I still believe everyone else was right, or would I see snakes differently? These thoughts were the inspiration behind "Amos the Snake."

✳ ✳ ✳

Amos was a young garter snake. And if you've ever seen a family of garter snakes, you know that Amos had plenty of brothers and sisters. Well, it didn't take Amos long to get tired of looking after his brothers and sisters all the time, so one day Amos decided he was going to run away and try to find a place where he could be alone and do just what he wanted. He decided he was going to leave in the middle of the night when everyone was sleeping. He lay down and pretended to be asleep until everyone in his hole had fallen into a deep slumber. Then, quiet as a mouse, Amos crawled out of the family hole into the night. He refused to look back because he was afraid he would change his mind. After he had been traveling through the woods for about an hour, he began to sense a storm coming up. "This is a fine time for me to run away," Amos thought to himself. He started looking around for shelter. He had crawled too far to return home before the storm started, and, anyway; he didn't want to run home at the first sign of trouble. He was braver than that.

He decided to climb a tree so he could get a better look at what was around him. As he climbed, he felt proud of how easily he managed to get up the tree. "There aren't many snakes my age who can climb a tree this good," he thought to himself. When he was almost to the top of the tree, he looked around to see what he could see. Just then he heard a chirping sound, but he couldn't see anything or anybody. He heard the sound again.

He began to grow frightened. He could sense something moving closer and closer. Slowly he inched his way down the tree, scared that if he started to run he would be killed for sure. He figured that if he could reach the ground first, maybe he could coil up and strike whatever it was or maybe even wrap himself around it and squeeze it. "Chirp, chirp!" There it was again, right behind him. Amos decided to make a break for it. He swiftly glided down the tree. When he reached the bottom, he coiled himself up, ready to strike whatever it was. He sat silently so he could strike at whatever he heard. It was still too dark to see anything. But whatever this thing was, it was following him. The only other sound Amos could hear was the distant rumbling of the storm. He was pretty scared now, and his whole body was tensed and ready. Why didn't it chirp anymore? Why was it so quiet? It couldn't have moved away, or he would have heard it. Just then a flash of lightning lit up the sky, and

Amos could see it, just about a foot above him up the tree, staring with its scary brown eyes. Before the sky became dark again, Amos made his move. He struck at it, and he hit it. He heard it hit the ground.

"Chirp, chirp, chirp!"

Amos crawled over to it. He was just about to wrap himself around it to finish it off when lightning lit the sky again. Now Amos could get a better look. Why, he couldn't believe his eyes! He had attacked a little baby squirrel.

"Chirp, chirp!"

The little squirrel was in pain and could hardly move. Amos was ashamed of himself. "Are you bad hurt?" asked Amos.

"I ... I can't move my legs," squeaked the little squirrel. "It hurts real bad."

"I thought you was going to hurt me," said Amos.

"I just wanted somebody to be with," said the squirrel. "You see, my mama was killed by a fox yesterday, and I'm all by myself."

Amos was so ashamed that he almost began to cry. "Lord, I'm sorry. I didn't know." Just then the rain started, sprinkling both Amos and the squirrel. "We got to find someplace out of the rain," said Amos.

"There's a tree trunk just over there," said the squirrel, motioning to his left, "but I don't think I can get to it."

"Don't worry," said Amos. "I'll help you." So Amos, ever so gently, helped the little squirrel to the trunk of the tree. As they sat in the tree watching the rain, Amos and the little squirrel began talking and soon became good friends. After a few days, the little squirrel's leg was better, and he could walk on it again. Well, Amos was becoming homesick now, and he knew his mama and daddy would be looking for him, so he decided to go home. The little squirrel began feeling very sad, because he had grown to love

Amos. As Amos was about to leave, he noticed the little squirrel's sadness and asked him what was wrong.

"I'm going to miss you," said the little squirrel. "I really like you, Amos."

"I like you too," said Amos, "but there's no need to say goodbye because you're going with me."

"Really?" said the little squirrel.

"Really," said Amos. "You can come and live with us. Of course, we'll have to find a tree and build you a proper nest, but we'll see each other every day, just like now."

"Oh boy," said the little squirrel. "I love you, Amos." The squirrel jumped on Amos and gave him a big hug, and they both started for home. And from that day to this, squirrels and garter snakes have been the best of friends.

TO BE FREE

Blacks made many efforts to fight their enslavement. From the attempts of Africans to run away upon landing in North America to the crusade of the abolitionists, blacks worked hard for their freedom. The stories in this chapter focus on attaining freedom and coping with its challenges.

In the colonial and antebellum periods, blacks were relegated to the status of property. The laws protected property owners and also sought to establish standards of behavior for slaves.

A slave had no standing in the courts. He could not bring suit, could not testify against a white, could not own property, and could not strike a white person. Running away or even stealing a hog was an offense punishable by death. Because of the possibility of insurrection and rebellion, blacks could not own or carry firearms, be in gatherings of two of more people without a white being around, or buy or sell goods without their masters' permission.

The punishment for breaking these laws could be thirty-nine lashes with a whip, dismemberment, branding, imprisonment, or death. In all slaveholding states, arson, rape of a white woman, rebellion, or conspiracy to rebel were punishable by death. A slave could also be "outlawed," or shot on sight. The local county or parish was responsible for reimbursing the owner for the value of the slave.

A slave's main protection from harm and mistreatment derived from appropriating information and using it wisely. Many blacks believed in the saying, "I have one face for you to see and one that is really me." They realized that it sometimes was advantageous to be someone else. Those blacks who succeeded in running away, received extra rations of food or clothing, and avoided being sold or having their loved ones sold were those with skills, knowledge, or positions within the owner's family that put them in a favored role.

African Americans showed enormous courage, determination, and imagination in working for freedom, often risking their lives. Stowaways hid on vessels, women disguised themselves as men, and mulattoes—biracial African Americans—posed as masters with their wives and children as their slaves. Enslaved African Americans contorted themselves in boxes and shipped themselves to freedom. They traveled by night and rested by day. They went without food or water for days. They suffered untold horrors and still pushed forward toward freedom. And when they were finally free, men and women like Sojourner Truth, Harriet Tubman, Henry "Box" Brown, Lewis Clark, and Frederick Douglass spoke out for the abolition of slavery. They published newspapers, wrote books, and contributed to countless narratives. ✹

Viney's Free Papers

I first heard a wonderful adaptation of Paul Laurence Dunbar's short story "The Sword of Gideon" by Dylan Pritchett, a good friend. Although Dunbar, one of the most beloved black poets of the nineteenth century, was not known for his short stories, "The Sword of Gideon" provided me with an opportunity to talk about the special magic that can occur when two people are in love, no matter what the circumstances. Even the oppressive nature of slavery did not keep Africans and African Americans from finding each other and falling in love.

✳ ✳ ✳

From the first time he saw her, Ben Raymond loved Viney. Although he was over six feet tall and as strong as any two workers on the plantation, he was scared stiff when it came to revealing his true feelings, especially about her. He first met Viney when she was sent to work in the tobacco fields where he was foreman.

From the moment he saw her, he wanted her for his own. She was as pretty as a picture and a hard worker. But what he liked most about her was her strength. She was small in size, but she had the strength of ten men in her spirit. No one took advantage of Viney, and Ben liked that. To survive as a slave, you had to be strong. With her at his side, he felt there was nothing he couldn't do.

But she was so bold and assertive that she also made him feel awkward. Whenever he was around her, his heart began beating fast, his palms started sweating, and his legs shook like tree limbs on a windy day. Sometimes he could just look at her and grow dizzy right on the spot! His mouth became as dry as cotton, and, even if he wanted to, he couldn't speak above a whisper.

He didn't like others to see him when he was around Viney because he acted so silly. And to be a good foreman, he had to convince everyone who worked for him that he was in control at all times.

In spite of these handicaps, the time had come to ask her to be his—or at least to try. He didn't want to lose her to some other young buck. Most of them didn't know how special she was, and she deserved someone who did.

He thought about her all the time. When he worked in the fields, when he chopped wood, when he was fixing the wagon wheels, even when he slept, she was on his mind.

One day he sent a note to Viney, asking her to meet him in the woods at dusk. She sent word back that she would be there.

He had arrived at the meeting place early, and he was pacing back and forth talking to himself, trying to decide what he was going to say to her. "Viney, I ... aw, that ain't it ... Viney, you ... Viney ... we ... naw! Viney you and me ... no, no, no."

Just about that time Viney arrived. "Ben Raymond, why you got me coming out here in these dark, scary woods this time of night?" asked Viney impatiently. "I was scared a snake or something was going to bite me."

"Well ... uh, uh, uh, uh ... I ... uh ... wanted to talk to you," said Ben in almost a whisper.

"What do you want to talk about?"

"Well ... well ... uh ... um ... um ... uh ... you know, I was plowing in the field the other day, and I was going along fine when all of a sudden, there in the furrow I was plowin' was a great big mess of black snakes. You should have seen the mama snake. She was all curled up ready to protect her young 'uns!" said Ben excitedly.

"Ben Raymond, do you think I like to hear snake stories?"

"No."

"Then why are you tellin' me one?" asked Viney, tapping one foot and rolling her eyes.

"That's not what I wanted to talk to you about," said Ben desperately. Petrified with fear, he shifted his weight to one side, shifted back again, and then stood stark still with one foot resting on the other.

"Well, what is it then?"

"Well um ... um ... um ... you know, Master Taylor's been looking real hard at me lately. And I don't think it's gon' be long before he'll have me working his mill directly. He knows I know everything there is to know about runnin' a gristmill. I think he'll ask me to do it full time pretty soon," said Ben, happy to have gotten it out and standing straighter because of his new-found voice.

"That's real nice, Ben Raymond."

"Yeah, I might even get to keep some of the tips I make," offered Ben.

"That's real nice, Ben."

"Yeah, I might even get to take a trip to Richmond one day," bragged Ben as he put his hands in his pockets and kicked a nearby twig.

"Now wait a minute, Ben," said Viney. "I don't know any master in these parts that would let a slave he owns go that far. What's to keep you from running away if you had a mind to?"

"You," said Ben in a soft voice.

"Me?" Viney said in surprise. Realizing that Ben had something serious in mind, she now became nervous. She turned her eyes from him, looked down at the ground and slid away demurely.

"Sit down there on that stump, Viney," Ben commanded.

Viney sheepishly obeyed. She tucked her ruffled skirt under her backside and sat down on the stump as if it were a fancy ladder-back chair.

"Now, you and me been knowing each other for clear past a year now, and I been lookin' at you, and I know you been lookin' at me!"

Ben was hitting his stride now, and he stared at her boldly as he let her know she had eyes for him too.

"Now wait a minute, Ben Raymond ...," cautioned Viney as she fumbled with the pleats in her skirt.

Ben broke in, "I ain't got time to make it pretty for ya' now! Don't neither one of us know when we may be sold clean from around here, so I figure whatever happiness we got, we might as well jump on it with both feet. I wants you for my wife, and I's fixin' to ask your master if you and me can't jump the broom.

"I don't know, Ben Raymond," Viney said shyly as she stood up and sashayed away from him.

"You know how I feel about you woman ... you know ... you know ... you know I ... uh ... you know ... love you." Ben managed an awkward smile in spite of his nervousness.

"Oh, do you, Ben Raymond?"

"Oh Lord, now she's gon' make it harder than it already is!" groaned Ben.

"I'm not trying to make it hard for you, Ben," said Viney. "I just want you to be sure about what you sayin'. This is the most I've heard you talk, 'cept when you're funnin' with the little children. I just want you to be sure about your feelings, that's all."

"You askin' me a whole lot of questions 'bout my feelings, but you ain't said nothin' 'bout yours yet."

"Ben Raymond," said Viney with her hands on her hips.

"How many men do you think I'd meet out here in these dark, scary woods at this time of night? How many, huh? I've had strong feelings for you ever since I seen you on that hay cart last June." She looked down at her shoes and twisted from side to side, completely vulnerable to anything he might say.

"Oh yeah?" said Ben, beaming with pride. "Well, what 'bout Hollis Price?"

"What about Hollis?" Viney responded defensively, bracing for an argument. "He's decent enough to say more than two words to me in public—which is more than I can say for *some* people."

"Well, I just don't like everybody knowin' my business," said Ben.

"Well, neither do I."

"Oh, is that why y'all always holding hands and looking goose-eyed at each other?" Ben looked directly in Viney's eyes.

Viney exploded. "I never looked goose-eyed at Hollis Price! Maybe you need to go to the apothecary shop and get some herbs for your eyes!" She shook her finger squarely in his face and stomped her feet furiously.

"My eyes work fine, and I know what I saw—and more than once too, Viney!" They were close enough to touch noses as Ben held his ground.

Seeing that he was not going to back down, Viney stomped away from him a few feet and decided to ask him a question that was even more important than what they were arguing about: "Did you come here to fuss at me or to ask me to marry you?"

Ben, realizing that he had lost his temper at the worst possible time, looked toward the ground. "I'm sorry," he said. Then, glancing around to make sure no one was watching, he sauntered over to Viney, slid his hand in her hand, pulled her close to him, and, ever so gently, he sealed their bond with a kiss.

Feeling a sense of accomplishment, Ben asked, "So, when

do you think is a good time for me to talk to your master?"

"Well," said Viney, "he counts his tobacco on Fridays, so he's in a good mood then. Talk to him on Friday."

"Friday it is then," said Ben. "But Viney, you ain't gon' change your mind, is you?" asked Ben, afraid that this was too good to be true.

"No, Ben Raymond," assured Viney. "You ain't gon' change yours, is you?"

"Not even if a whole big mess of black snakes curled up and started after me with their fangs just awaitin' to sink into my legs!" teased Ben.

"Ben Raymond!" screamed Viney. "You know I'm afraid of snakes!" She chased him around in a circle, fussing at him as she ran. They both had a good laugh as they realized that their time together was growing short. They kissed one last time and parted.

Ben floated home that night. It was as if he were walking on a cloud. All he could see ahead of him were images of Viney and himself kissing each other goodbye. He had finally done it!

Soon after that night, Viney and Ben Raymond were married. Viney's mother brought a special broom made of corn shucks and laid it down behind them. Just as the preacher said they were married, they turned around and jumped over the broom together. Ben had finally done it. Viney was now a permanent part of his life.

After they were married, Ben Raymond took his new bride home. He had built a small twelve-by-fifteen-foot cabin for them to live in.

As time passed he did what he could to make the cabin a home for Viney. One year he made a chest of drawers for her that he placed in one corner. Another year he made a bedstead for her so they wouldn't have to sleep on the floor like most of the other slaves. He also made her a rocking chair, placing it in a special spot in the house so she could rest herself after a hard day's work.

All around the house were things that proved to Viney how much Ben Raymond loved her and wanted to care for her.

And they were happy. Aw, they were happy! Whenever other slaves on the quarter were depressed, as they often were, feeling as if no one cared, they'd visit Viney and Ben Raymond's place. They were sure to leave there feeling better about themselves and armed with a bit of wisdom that would get them through the rest of their week.

Ben Raymond promised Viney one thing before they were married: He promised her he would purchase her freedom. In those days, if you were free, you had to have papers proving it, and those papers had to be with you at all times or you could be sold back into slavery.

Viney was owned by Master John Taylor. He had owned her for about seven years, and since he had approved their broomstick marriage, he knew it wouldn't be long before Ben would be coming to ask him to draw up free papers for Viney.

Both men settled on a price of two hundred dollars. Ben figured it would take him at least four years to earn that kind of money.

Every day and every season when he had finished the master's work, he'd take on extra tasks. He was a good carpenter, so he'd take on odd jobs and work half the night sometimes to earn a few dollars a week.

During the winter months, he'd work in the cold. One time he almost cut his leg clean off, chopping up a load of wood for a widower who lived nearby, but he never complained. He knew he was doing it all for his beloved Viney.

Days turned into weeks, weeks to months, and months to years.

Finally, after five long years, Ben Raymond had two hundred dollars—enough money to buy Viney's free papers.

It was in the fifth anniversary of their marriage.

That morning he got up bright and early and made as little noise as he could. He didn't want to wake Viney, not just yet.

He went to a corner of the room where he had placed five short pieces of wood into dirt the floor of their cabin. He had dug a hole in the floor and made a small root cellar where he put his valuables. This is where he kept the money he had been saving. He gathered up the money, holding it as if it were a newborn child, replaced the logs covering the cellar, and started out the door.

As he walked across the field to Master Taylor's house, some of the slaves were already up and working. One saw Ben Raymond and noticed the money in his hands.

He said, "Look, there's Ben Raymond. He's headed to the master's house with a whole handful of money. Today must be the day."

Everybody on the quarter knew that Ben was saving to buy Viney's freedom. They knew how long and hard he had worked for that money, and they all respected him for it. After all, there weren't too many men who would be that faithful for five long years.

"Hey, Ben Raymond, is today the day?" yelled a slave.

Ben Raymond didn't speak. He just looked straight ahead and carried that money ever so gently to Master Taylor.

When he reached Master Taylor's house, he knocked on the door. Master Taylor himself opened it.

John Taylor was a slave owner, but he was also a Christian who believed that all people should be treated respectfully. Taylor knew Ben was a special man. All the slaves respected him because he was respectful of them, not because he was bigger and stronger and had the power to punish them, but because they were human beings and part of his extended family, Ben knew how to handle all the workers, from the youngest to the oldest.

So when Ben asked Master Taylor if he could buy his wife's

freedom, it was very hard for the slave owner to refuse.

He looked knowingly at Ben. "Is today the day, Ben?"

"Yessuh," said Ben. "Today is the day."

Taylor took Ben into the parlor where he had already prepared the free papers. All that was left to do was sign them. He picked up his quill pen, dipped it in a small jar of ink, and signed his name. After he signed the papers, he put his seal on them and presented them to Ben.

Ben Raymond handed Taylor the two hundred dollars, saying, "You can count it. I got it all right here."

"No need, Ben. You been saving for five years. I reckon you know these dollar bills personally by now. And there's no doubt in my mind that all of the money is here."

"Thank you, suh," Ben said triumphantly.

He walked toward the door. Master Taylor himself opened the door and let Ben out.

As Ben walked back toward the quarter, it seemed that all the slaves had gathered at the end of the row to get a look at the free papers.

"That's them," said one. "Them's the free papers. Ben Raymond, you got 'em, you got 'em. I knowed you would."

Ben Raymond said nothing. He just walked toward his cabin. When he arrived at the door, he quietly opened it and called to Viney.

"Viney, Viney my darlin', wake up."

Slowly Viney opened her eyes and sat up in the bed.

"I got something for you," he said.

"What is it?"

He handed her the papers. She looked at them and asked, "What do they say, Ben Raymond?"

"They says you's free. They says you can go anywhere and do anything you want to do. You's free now."

Viney looked at the papers and she looked at Ben, and she looked at the papers not knowing whether to laugh, cry, scream, pray, or jump for joy.

She looked at Ben and immediately realized that it was his hard work and dedication that had allowed this to happen, so she reached out and gave Ben a great big hug.

She hugged him hard and she hugged him long. In fact, they hugged and kissed for the rest of that day. Even when Ben was out in the field tending to the work gang, Viney would kiss and hug him every chance she got.

The next morning, Viney got up and took her papers around the other quarters so that all the others could see that she was a free woman. "Look what my Ben did for me," she said proudly. "I's as free as anybody now. I can go anywhere I please and do anything I please!"

The next day she decided to go into town to show all of the other free blacks there that she was now one of them. Many times she had seen them on trips to town. As they did with most bond-men and bondwomen, free blacks looked down their noses at her. Well, now, she was one of them. She went into town and stayed the entire day.

Next day—no Viney. The next day—no Viney.

Ben Raymond became concerned after she didn't return the second day. Even if she had gone to one of the stores to look at the fancy new dresses, she should have been back by the second day.

There were night patrols in those days that blacks knew as "patterollers." Blacks were afraid of the patterollers because they often treated blacks badly and accused them of trying to run away, just so they could collect a handsome reward. They could even abuse them without fear of retribution by the slave owners, so most blacks stayed out of their way.

What if Viney had been stopped by some of them? Ben

didn't even want to think of what might happen.

Then too, he thought, maybe she had fallen ill. Maybe she had hurt herself and was somewhere in the woods unable to move or scream for help.

Desperate to find out where she was, he sent word to town, asking his friends to contact him if they knew of her whereabouts.

In a matter of hours, word came back from one of the drivers on a neighboring farm that he'd seen her and she was all right. He said she was in town and that she was spending a great deal of time with some of the free blacks there.

On the morning of the fifth day, the door to Ben's cabin opened and in walked Viney. Ben Raymond sprang up from the rocking chair he'd been sitting in for the last five days and began, "Viney Raymond, where have you ..."

Viney stopped him in mid-sentence. "Ah, ah, ah, my name is Viney Allen now. I'm free, and I'm leaving you, Ben Raymond. I hear there are lots of free blacks in Baltimore, and I'm going to Baltimore so I can be with them."

She walked over to the chest of drawers and began packing her clothes. But before she could finish, the door opened and Hollis Price walked through.

"You ready, Viney?" he asked.

"Hollis, you wait for me outside," she answered.

She finished her packing and turned to leave. Before she walked out the door, she decided to take one more look at the house, and her eyes fell on the chest of drawers.

She remembered the week Ben had worked on the drawers. He wanted to make them out of walnut, so they'd be nice and sturdy and look pretty as well. Those drawers had to close just right. Ben couldn't stand anything that was done halfway. It had to be the best he could do. That was just the way he was.

Then she looked at the bedstead. No other slaves in the

quarters slept up off the ground like that, but Ben had told her he wanted her to sleep as the white folks slept.

Then she looked at the rocking chair. Ben had made that out of tulip poplar. He had gone down to the James River one night to cut that poplar down and nearly suffered frostbite. He'd gotten splinters all in his hands and a sore back from dragging that old tree to the house, but he wanted to make that chair just so for her.

She looked all around the room, and everywhere she looked, she saw evidence of Ben Raymond's love for her.

She took out her free papers and said, "It's these damn papers, ain't it?"

Before Ben could say or do anything, she crossed over to the fireplace and threw in the papers.

"No, no, no!" said Ben. "Don't do that, Viney!"

"I don't want no free papers," Viney yelled. "I don't want no papers—if it means I have to be without you."

For the first time in a long time, the old Viney was back with him. Ben Raymond grabbed her, and they hugged and kissed for the rest of that day. Since it was Sunday, their one day off, they could just enjoy each other's company all day long.

The next morning Ben Raymond got up and went to Master Taylor and told him the story about Viney's free papers. Master Taylor took him into the parlor and drew up another set of papers. They weren't as fancy as the first ones, but they were just as legal. He handed them to Ben. Ben thanked him, shook his hand, and left.

He took the papers to Viney and presented them to her, but Viney pushed the papers back to Ben and said, "You keep them. And the next time I act like I don't know who I am, or like I don't love you, just take these papers and tear them up."

Many years passed, and Viney and Ben Raymond enjoyed happiness for most of them, even though neither of them lived to see emancipation.

But from the day Viney came back to Ben until the day she died, Ben Raymond never had to touch those free papers again. From that day on, Viney understood the meaning of true freedom.

The Runaway

Another kind of hero from the 1780s and 1790s represents the thousands of Africans and African Americans who decided to free themselves by running away. These brave men and women put themselves in danger and did so at a time when there was no real freedom "up North." It took special courage for these African Americans to expose themselves to the perils that lurked around every tree and over the top of every hill. It also took some planning if an escape were to be successful. Here's the story of one such person, who found out that freedom was much more than a simple notion.

✵ ✵ ✵

Titus was tired. Tired of sweating, tired of bending over cow dung, tired of his back aching, and tired of grown-ups telling him he was working too slowly.

He had turned fourteen just two days earlier, and no one had wished him a happy birthday or even acted as if it were a special day for him. He didn't expect everyone on the quarter to know, but he did think Aunt Lizzy would remember. She was his only kin since they had sold his mother and father away. She wasn't really his aunt. He just called her that because she treated him like he was one of the family. She always looked out for him and made sure no one took advantage of him, especially when she was around.

Only two months earlier he had been given the quota of a full hand. Master Rollins said he was big and strong enough to do a man's work, so they took him from the kitchen and the big house and put him to work in the fields.

Working the field was hard. When he worked with Mandy and the others in the house, it wasn't so bad. He carried water, kept fires lit, cut and fetched firewood, cleaned windows, whitewashed fences, scrubbed floors, and helped with the laundry. He could do a variety of things, so he didn't get bored, and he could always take a break when he became tired. Sometimes Mandy would make ginger cake or blackberry pie, and she always let him have the first piece. No one whipped him in the house as they did in the fields. No one ever stood over him, from sunup to sundown, and watched every move he made.

Titus disliked everything about field work. The cow dung they used to fertilize the tobacco hills smelled something awful. The sun was so hot it seemed to burn his skin right to the bone. Before the sun was even at its peak, sweat dripped off of him, making him look as if he had fallen in the creek. Flies, mosquitoes, chiggers, red bugs, ticks, and gnats kept him slapping at his skin all day long.

And there was never enough fresh water to go around. By the time the water boy got to Titus, it always seemed that there was none left. Then he had to wait for them to fetch more water. Sometimes his throat was so parched he felt as if he had been drinking dust.

There was no real shade to speak of. All the trees had been removed. Every inch of the field was used to plant the almighty tobacco.

The best part of the day was lunch. Cornbread, hickory-smoked bacon, hominy, and maybe even a hoecake with molasses for dessert. But no matter how much food he ate in the fields, it never tasted as good as the food that Mandy prepared, because that was food for the master and his family. Roasted chicken, fresh vegetables from the garden, wheat bread, potatoes, apple or peach pie. Thinking about all that food made his mouth water.

"Get back to work, or I'll come over there with this cat," yelled Jasper, the overseer, brandishing a short multistranded whip called a cat-o'-nine-tails. "Every time I look your way, you're daydreaming about something. I bet I can stop you from doing that! You keep it up and I'll show you how! You ain't in the kitchen no more with them house hands. We do real work out here!"

"Boy, you'd better git to stepping on that row or your aunt will be making poultices for your raw backside," warned Cyrus.

Cyrus was the only real friend Titus had since they had put him in the field. "After Ol' Jasper finish with you, you'll be lucky if you able to stand."

"I hate being here. I hate the overseer and I hate being a slave!" said Titus.

"If you don't shut your mouth, that overseer gon' hear you, and he'll give you a pain that'll make you wish you had never been born!" said Ol' Jim. Jim was the oldest worker in the field. Most of the blacks at the quarter had more respect for him than they did for the white overseer. They knew that Jim, who remembered things about Africa, the old country, only wanted what was best for them. But Titus hadn't learned that yet.

"Now, you ain't been out here long, but you better know right now that when you acts like you doing now, you make it bad for all of us. That overseer wants us to work together and shut our mouths. As long as we don't give him trouble and do our work, he leaves us alone and spares the cat-o'-nine-tails. You ain't just putting yourself in danger, you putting every last one of us in danger too."

Still angry and sullen, Titus said, "I'm a git outta here. I'm a run away." *Wham!* Ol' Jim reached over and slapped Titus square across the face. He hit him so hard that Titus fell to the soft, plowed ground with a thud. "What you hit me for?" yelled Titus, tears starting to well in his eyes.

Ol' Jim didn't say a word. He just turned and walked back toward his row and continued his work.

Jasper had seen it all, and he almost burst his sides laughing. "Looks like Ol' Jim got to you before I did, didn't he? If you don't straighten up, what he did to you will seem small compared to what I'm gon' do. Ha, ha, ha, ha!"

Cyrus helped Titus up as they both watched the overseer ride off on his horse. "You got to watch what you say, fool!" said Cyrus. "You don't mention running away in mixed company, even if everybody does look like you and me. Don't you know Ol' Jasper can whip you to death for even saying something like that? And the master would give him a reward instead of a punishment.

"You got to learn that there's ways to act when you work in the big house and other ways to act when you out here. And the best way to git yourself sold off or whipped nearly to death is to even mention running away in mixed company."

Titus brushed himself off and quietly went back to work. He didn't speak to anyone for the rest of the day. But in his mind—where no one could hear his thoughts—he had promised himself that the first chance he got, he was going to run away.

Finally the sun went down behind the trees and the overseer called it a day. Titus was so tired that he didn't even know if he could make it back to Aunt Lizzy's cabin. He didn't even have an appetite. "I'll just eat a little something and lay on my pallet. I need to rest. Every bone in my body is aching," he mumbled to himself as he headed toward Aunt Lizzy's.

When he arrived at the cabin, Aunt Lizzy had a pot of hominy waiting. He took the gourd dipper, scooped himself a bowl full, and headed to his pallet to eat. Aunt Lizzy said she had to go out for a minute and she'd be back before he finished his hominy.

For a few minutes, he had the cabin to himself. He looked into the fireplace and said to himself, "We sure don't need a fire in here as hot as it is." But Aunt Lizzy always had a fire in the fireplace and a pot of something hanging in it.

He knew that she did that because there were times when others around the quarter would come and ask for food. Some of the slaves had more mouths to feed than a peck of corn would handle for a week. That was the ration that all of them got. For some it was OK, but for others it wasn't nearly enough, so she did what she could to help those who needed more.

The fire in the fireplace was hypnotic, and Titus's eyes started to droop. Before long, he had drifted off to sleep.

He began dreaming about wide open fields, wind blowing through the trees, and birds chirping. Everywhere he looked in his dream, he saw birds, all kinds of birds flying high in the sky. Some floated on the wind; others flapped their wings; others sat in the top of trees and sang their songs of joy. They seemed so happy with nothing to do except fly around the heavens all day.

As he looked up into a particularly large tree, he saw a great big bird. It looked like a hawk. As he walked closer to the tree, the bird seemed to be looking down at him. The bird seemed to be chirping his name. "Titus, Titus, Titus, Titus." The bird chirped his name more loudly. Suddenly he felt a hand on his shoulder.

It was Aunt Lizzy trying to wake him up! "Titus, get up, honey. I know you're tired but I got something for you." Titus sat up and noticed there was someone else in the room. It was Mandy, the master's cook and his good friend, and she held a blackberry pie in her hand!

"I wanted to give this to you the day your Aunt Lizzy asked for it, but Master Rollins was here for a couple of days and when he's around, it is hard for me to bake anything that's not for him.

And he does love my blackberry pies. But I made this one special for you. Happy birthday, honey. I know it's late a-comin', but I hope you enjoy it just the same."

Titus stood up from his pallet, walked over to Mandy, took the pie, set it near the fireplace, and gave Mandy the biggest hug he could. Then he went to Aunt Lizzy and gave her one too.

"Thank you, thank you both," said Titus. "I thought everybody had forgot."

"Now, why would we do that?" asked Aunt Lizzy. "Who could forget the day the Lord brought you into this world? Your mama said you screamed at the top of your lungs for a whole day before you calmed down.

"She told me, when she left you with me, you was gon' be a handful. She said you had grit in your craw and that she didn't want anybody beatin' it out of you. Said you had courage and she hoped I'd be able to help you balance your courage with good sense. I'm still working on it, ha, ha, ha, ha! Now let's cut that pie and see if Mandy still got the touch."

Just then someone knocked on the door, and in walked Cyrus, Daisey, and Ol' Jim. "I told you that was blackberry pie I smelled," bragged Cyrus.

"Yep, you were right," said Ol' Jim. "Mind if we come in and join ya'?"

"It's Titus's pie, so it's Titus's decision. What do you say, Titus?" asked Aunt Lizzy.

Titus wanted to tell Cyrus and Daisey they could stay—but not Ol' Jim. He remembered only too well what Jim had done earlier in the field, and he didn't want to share his pie with that ol' mule—not one bite. But he knew that wasn't the Christian thing to do, so he said, "Come on in. There's plenty."

Aunt Lizzy cut the pie, and everyone sat around the fireplace enjoying Mandy's pie.

After a while the room became quiet and Daisey started singing a song. They all sat and listened to her mournful tune. She had such a lovely voice, and when she sang, it was as if she took her listeners to another world.

Titus looked over at Ol' Jim and saw in a minute that he was crying. He nudged Aunt Lizzy, motioning in Ol' Jim's direction.

Aunt Lizzy waited a few minutes, giving him time to get himself together, and then, with the greatest of care, she asked him what was wrong. Daisey stopped her song, but Ol' Jim asked her to hum a little bit of it, and he began to speak.

"I slapped your boy today in the field, Lizzy. Did he tell you?"

"No," answered Lizzy, "not a word."

"Well I did. I know he don't know why, so I'll tell you now." Daisey continued her humming.

"A while back, I had a son who was a lot like you, Titus. Headstrong, full of himself, and brazen. He hated being what we all is, and each day he worked in the fields was a day he felt like he was in hell. I tried to talk to him, but every time I said something to him about being a good worker and how important it was to keeping us together as a family, he'd walk away without a word. One day he walked away, and I got mad at his disrespectful ways, so I slapped him across his face.

"He looked at me, and his eyes looked dead. It was like he had no feelings for me or anybody or anything. He didn't try to hit me back. He didn't even act like my hitting him meant anything. He said nothing to me, his mama, or his brothers and sisters. He didn't speak to me for three whole days. He wouldn't eat, and he worked harder in those three days than he had in three years.

"On the evening of the fourth day, which was a Sunday, he got up early in the morning, opened the cabin door, and walked out. I thought he was just headed back to the privy, but it took him so long to come back, I sent one of the others to check on him. He was long gone. With only the clothes on his back, he'd run off.

"I ain't heard from him since. In my mind I want to believe he got away and is somewhere doing fine. But at night, when I'm layin' on my pallet alone, I fears he's been dragged off somewhere and shot. He wouldn't have just gone and not tried to send us a message. I fears the patterollers got him and did Lord knows what.

"So today, when you said what you did, I just couldn't take it. Just didn't want you to be like my boy. I know you's miserable out in that field. We all is. But at least we's in the land of the livin' and we's together. It ain't much, but it's somethin'.

"Now hear me right, boy. I ain't sayin' don't run away. I's sayin', don't just wake up one morning and walk off. You do that, and who knows what will happen. If you serious 'bout leaving, and God knows it's the youngsters that stand the best chance of making it stick, you'd better give it some real thinking time."

"I knew the time would come when you'd git that feeling to run, but I didn't think it would be for a while, chile!" moaned Aunt Lizzy. "Why would you do something like that, Titus? Ain't I treated you like one of my own?"

"Ain't got nothing to do with you, Aunt Lizzy. I just don't want to be in that field anymore. I'm tired, just tired," said Titus. "But, like Uncle Jim say, I don't have to do it right this minute. I just needs to bide my time and get me in some real thinkin' time. Right, Uncle Jim?"

"Now you talking like you somebody with some sense. Just take your time. We'll all help you and tell you what you needs for to have the best chance of makin' it stick," said Ol' Jim. "But until then, just act like everything is normal. And control your mouth when you in that field and 'round that overseer. Now, is there any more of that pie left? I'd like another hunk!"

"Comin' just as quick as I can git it," said Mandy.

"Daisey, sing a song that we can all join in with," Aunt Lizzy said, smiling.

As they all sang a song by the light of the fireplace, Titus thought to himself, Ol' Jim wasn't really an old mule—he was a fox.

AIN'T GWINE STUDY WAR NO MORE

This chapter focuses on those nameless heroines who didn't become nationally known but represent the strength, courage, and unwavering spirit it took to seek the best out of the worst, and dared to hope for better days for themselves and those they loved.

After slavery, African-American women were forced to raise their children without the help of a father. This happened for several reasons. First, many slave owners had broken up black families when they sent males off to work in other areas for extended periods. Second, black men and women had served at the pleasure of the owner and had to do as they were told. Families often had been separated in the process. Third, whites owned lands in locations throughout a county, and many teams of slaves had often been sent to outlying areas to tend land for long periods.

These separations put great stress on the women and children left behind. Even after emancipation, internal and external pressures challenged the black family. Mothers attempted to provide guidance to children who had no models to teach them how to deal with their new freedom. Black families also had to confront terrible social, economic, and political pressures: white racism intensified, jobs for blacks were scarce, wages were poor, and blacks often had little or no education. Young blacks struggled to create new identities in their own communities, as many vied for the same jobs and competed for the same opportunities. All of this left mothers continually fighting an uphill battle as they tried to help their children adjust to a new life. ✳

Emancipation Day

The emancipation of blacks began as early as 1861, the year the Civil War began, and in 1862 Washington, D.C., and the United States territories banned slavery. That same year, the Confiscation Act granted freedom to all slaves whose masters supported the Confederacy. On January 1, 1863, the Emancipation Proclamation took effect, but it did not affect thirteen parishes in Louisiana, forty-eight counties in West Virginia, seven counties in eastern Virginia, and all of the so-called border states. It did free slaves "in states that were in rebellion against the Union."[1] This was known as Emancipation Day in most black communities throughout the South. Many blacks, however, did not find out that emancipation had occurred until weeks and months after January first. In some states like Texas, a state that was still in rebellion against the Union, the word didn't get to the general black population until June when Union soldiers physically occupied Confederate properties. To this day, Texas still celebrates Juneteenth Day to mark emancipation. This story discusses the challenges blacks faced as they dealt with emancipation.

[1] Sharon Haley, *The Timetables of African-American History*. New York: Simon and Schuster, 1995, 148.

* * *

It was a day like any other in Southampton County, Virginia. May flies were already out and it was hardly past April. If it wasn't raining, then they were drenched with sweat from working in the cotton fields all day or from the sun beating down on them, pounding the top of their heads like a hammer.

No one wanted to be in those fields. A person had to be crazy to even come out there, not to mention walking in the mud and slush with bare feet. But there they were.

"Uh, oh," said Caesar. "Here comes Master Jasper. Wonder what we done now. He never comes out here unless there's something terrible wrong."

"Look at that sour look he's got on his face. I bet he gon' make it rough for somebody," said Cyrus.

"Well, it sure won't be me," said Caesar. "I ain't done nothin' for a change."

"I wonder if he found out Simon took that ham from the smokehouse yesterday," said Cyrus.

"Maybe he's mad because the crops ain't looking good and he don't stand to make much money. Maybe the mistress and he had another fight and he lost again. Maybe he's just plain mad 'cause he wants to be," said Caesar.

Carl Jasper was a small farmer who owned three slaves. But since it was planting time, he needed more help, so he had hired in two slaves from a nearby farm. Simon, Cyrus, and Caesar belonged to Jasper, and Clara and Joseph were hired in. Clara and Joseph were husband and wife. But even though Clara was a woman, she was still expected to do a man's work in the field.

As Jasper approached them, they all stopped their work and stiffened their bodies. "Well," whispered Cyrus, "he ain't got a whip in his hand, so I don't guess we gon' git the lash."

"Oh Lord, what we done now," moaned Clara. She was scared especially because she was a woman and she didn't want Jasper to drag her back to his house for sport. Joseph swore he'd kill the next man who tried that, black or white. Just seeing Jasper approach was enough to start Clara shaking.

"Simmer down, Clara," said Caesar. "You a hired hand. He ain't gon' do nothin' to you 'cause then he'll have to answer to your master."

"Yeah," said Simon, "and old Master Boone is worse than Jasper ever was."

"And that's a fact," agreed Joseph.

Cyrus spoke up, "We ain't done nothin' but weed these beans. We ain't had time for nothin' else. I wish he'd leave us be. White folks don't know how to just leave us be!"

"Clara, if there's trouble, you stand behind me," ordered Joseph.

"I ain't done nothin', Joseph. Ain't no use in hidin' behind you looking guilty," said Clara.

"Suit yourself, but I means what I say. He put his hands on you, and I'm gon' use this hoe for what it wasn't meant for," warned Joseph.

Caesar, trying to ease the building tension, called to Jasper loudly, "How you today, Master Jasper?" Jasper didn't respond to Caesar. Instead he nodded his head at them all and said, "All y'all gather round here. I needs to talk." They all put their hoes down and pushed in close to Jasper.

"I'm s'pose to tell y'all that the war ain't over but Lincoln done signed a proclamation to set you all free."

No one said a word. A long, dead silence hung in the air. They all looked at each other and finally Caesar spoke.

"You havin' fun with us, ain't you, Master? We goin' on

back to work now." They all reached for their hoes and turned toward the field.

"I ain't funnin' you and this ain't no joke," said Jasper. "You all is free and you can do what you please."

They all looked at each other and realized for the first time that it must be true. After another long pause, Cyrus asked, "What we gon' do now?"

Jasper jumped in, "You can all go swimmin' or you can all go to hell. It's your choice. I done said what I s'pose to say. Anybody ask you, you tell them I done what I was s'pose to do. You hear?"

"Yes sir," answered Simon. "We hear you."

Jasper turned and walked away with the same surly attitude he had when he arrived.

"That's one mean white man," said Clara. "Don't think I ever seen him smile."

"This ain't no smilin' day for him," Caesar said. "This is smilin' day for us. We free! We free!"

Simon began clapping his hands together and they all joined him. Then Simon began a rapid succession of hand clapping that alternated with knee slapping, chest slapping, shoulder, thigh, and even face slapping. It created a syncopated rhythm so infectious that the rest of the men began to dance in the muddy fields.

"Go, Simon, go!" said Clara jubilantly. "Hambone, hambone, where you been?"

And they all answered, "Round the world and back again."

Then Clara sang, "Hambone, hambone, where you bound?"

And they answered again, "Way down yonder on freedom's ground!"

They all danced and made up their own verses as they cavorted jubilantly in the muddy field.

As they danced, some fell in the mud and others turned cartwheels. All the while, Simon slapped hambone like a man possessed.

They frolicked this way until, exhausted, they sat down in a grassy spot close to the end of the row they had been working in.

"Don't even sound right, do it? We's free. My Lordy, have mercy. Free!" said Cyrus.

Joseph and Clara began dancing with one another again. The rest joined them again as Simon patted hambone. Joseph stopped again and crossed over to a dry spot to sit down. They all joined him. As they sat, drinking in the moment, Joseph's expression changed from one of joy to one of concern.

Simon, noticing this, asked, "What's wrong, Joseph? This is a celebration. You ought to be as happy as a pig in a potato patch."

"Cyrus was right. What we gon' do now?" asked Joseph. "All our lives, we depended on the master for everything. He give us food; he treat us when we sick; he tell us what to think; he tell us when to rest. Now we got to do it all. I don' know any life but this life."

"Joseph, you can do anything you wants to do," said Caesar. "You heard Massa Jasper."

Cyrus broke in, "Stop callin' him that! He ain't the massa no more. I don't know 'bout y'all, but I'm gittin' my few things and I'm leaving here right this minute—naw, I ain't even gon' go back to the quarter. He might change his mind. Y'all comin'?"

"I'm right in your shadow, man," said Simon. "Let's foot it on out of here. Clara, y'all comin'?"

"What should we do, Clara?" asked Joseph.

Clara remained silent, waiting for him to make a decision.

After a long pause Joseph said, "Ain't nothin' out there for us. Y'all go on."

"Ain't nothing for you here, either," said Caesar. "I know

you ain't as young as we are, but there's nothin' here but more slavin' for you, Joseph. Don't Clara deserve better than that?"

"Where you going, Caesar? And what you gon' do when you get there?" asked Joseph. "He setting you free, but he didn't give you nothing else. How you gon' make your living now? You free—yeah, free to starve to death. We got to think this through. I don't want to spend my life working and then, when I'm set free, die of starvation 'cause I can't earn enough for me and Clara."

"Joseph, I been with you nigh on ten years. Don't make me choose 'tween you and freedom," said Clara. "Don't make me do that."

"Come on, Clara. You can go with us," said Simon.

"Now you look here, Simon, I may be in disagreement with Joseph, but I ain't leavin' him just yet. We got lots of talkin' to do befo' that happens."

"I may be old but I can still take this hoe and crack your skull, Simon. Get your hands off her and keep them off," warned Joseph.

"Joseph, you don't have to do this. Both of you are our friends. Simon just wanted to help. That's all."

"If I'm wrong, then I'm apologizing to you, Simon," said Joseph.

"No need," replied Simon. "We all family here."

Clara walked away deep in thought and then said, "I don't want to go anywhere without you, Joseph, but I been waitin' for freedom all my life. My mama never saw it. Neither did my daddy or any of my kin. I feel like I owe it to them to smell freedom. To walk, eat, drink, and sleep free, but I can't do that here. This place smells like the master's place. It feels like I'm in chains here. I don't know what I'll do, but I'll do it as a free woman, and I'd like to do it with you. Let's leave this place for good."

"You the most irritatin' woman in these parts, you know

that? Let's get on out of here before I change my mind," said Joseph.

"Lead the way, boys," said Clara. "But you'd better step live-ly, because I got so much energy, I feel like I could fly away from this place with all of you under my arms."

"Let's get on out of here and taste some of that freedom," added Joseph. Clara grabbed Joseph's hand, and they all walked out of the fields, toward North and freedom.

> *"And before I'll be a slave, I'll be buried in my grave*
> *and go home to my lord and be free."*

The Prodigal Son

The Bible speaks of the prodigal son. In that story, an arrogant son leaves his father's house to make it on his own. After many misfortunes, the son realizes that the most important things in life are a loving family and home. Although the story of the prodigal son is ancient, errant sons have continued to exist throughout the centuries, a source of concern for those who love them. They have caused many tears for mothers who have tried everything to persuade them to change their ways and sleepless nights for fathers who have blamed themselves for not being able to reach out to their sons.

Here's a story within a poem about one anonymous author's desire to help others avoid the pain and suffering that wayward children can cause.

* * *

When I was in eighth grade, a math teacher named Jeffrey Williams recited a poem to me. We had finished our math, it was the end of the school year, and we had some time to kill. He asked the class if anyone had any poems they wanted to share. Now here was a man who knew math so well that he taught it. I would always sit in the back of the class, hoping he wouldn't call on me. I was terrified of math. What came to so many of my friends as simple concepts were so hard for me that I had convinced myself I could not do math, and that, worse, I'd never be able to conquer it. So I dreaded Mr. Williams's class. He would put an algebraic problem on the board and flash through the steps. It was like moving through air for him; it was like struggling through quicksand for me.

But that one day when we put the math books aside and he asked about the poetry was a day I will never forget. I had been a poet since first grade. I always received a copy of the "Best in the County" poem books because I always submitted a poem that was published, thus becoming recognized as one of the best young poets in the county. Poetry was my math. It was my moving through air. Here was the man I feared the most offering me a chance to change his perception of me by letting me do something in his class that he didn't have to explain to me over and over again. I jumped at the chance and recited one of my poems to the class. He seemed impressed, but then he did something I never would have expected. He recited a poem. It forever changed my jaundiced opinion of his ability as a teacher. The poem moved me so much that I committed it to memory that night. It seemed to express all of the same sentiments I knew many mothers in my neighborhood felt as they tried to deal with their sons. Mr. Williams had learned it when he was a boy, and he never knew who the author was.

For me, it was also important because it spoke in a language, syntax, and rhythm that obviously came from the black experience. That meant I didn't have to translate it into my experience as we had to do with most of the poetry, prose, and plays that we studied in English class. That also meant that the poem established vivid and undeniable images for those who one day would hear me tell it. Mr. Williams called it "The Dying Boy's Mistake."

The Dying Boy's Mistake

I have a sad, sad story to tell you,
and I hope that you will take it in
for it is a warning unto the nation
and especially to young men.
Boys, I hope you will sit and listen
to this story as it is said,
for it came from the lips of a sick boy
who was on his dying bed.
He called his mother to his bedside
to listen to his plea.
He said, "Mom, I hope no boy has ever
lived a life like me.
Mother, you tried to raise me
in a good old Christian way,
but I never loved the church people
and their old-timey ways.
Mornings you'd give me money
to put in Sunday school,
but I lost it in an alley crap game,
though I knew it was against your rule.
I studied my Sunday school lessons
sitting around an old crap game,
so that when I returned home,
I could tell about Jesus' name.

Mother, tell the boys to live the life
and don't try to be a fake.
I'm on my dying bed,
and I've made a great mistake.

I've spent many days and nights
drinking whiskey and swallowing gin.
I thought those days were sweet.
I thought they'd never end.
Mother, I had you fooled.
You thought I was living my best,
but I've eaten many things
to keep you from smelling my whiskey breath.
I've danced and frolicked;
worldly things I did not dread,
but after all what did they profit me?
I'm on my dying bed.
The boys would come to see me;
they would knock at my door.
I mean I then kept ready;
I was always ready to go.
They would come to see me
when I was well and upon my feet.
You could hear them whistling and calling
way down on the street.
They won't even drop me a postcard now
to see how I'm getting along.
They realize that my health is bad,
and they know that my money is gone.
But mother, I'm dying ...
The room grows dark and cold.
I've kept up with the world
but today I'm losing my soul.
It seems as if I can hear the angels saying,
Too late, too late, too late.'
It's not your fault, dear mother,
but my own, great mistake."

A Mother's Love
for Mary Carter Smith

This story is written in honor of Mary Carter Smith, the cofounder of the National Association of Black Storytellers and a master storyteller. She has been an inspiration to many African-American storytellers as we strive to be the best we can be. She—along with Linda Goss, Jackie Torrence, Brother Blue, Alice McGill, Augusta Baker, Spoon Williams, and many other elders—were telling stories about the African and African-American experience long before doing so became popular. Mary Carter Smith's courage, strength, love, and faith are an example to all storytellers who seek to live the lessons of the stories they tell.

✳ ✳ ✳

What's the strongest feeling in the world? Some say hate, some say fear, others say jealousy, while still others say greed. In those years after slavery, some declared it was loneliness. Sometimes freed men and women felt as if they were slaves without masters.

Freedom was a curious enterprise during the last quarter of the nineteenth century and the first quarter of the twentieth. While freedom for slaves had become the law of the land, after the Fourteenth Amendment, the lives of ex-slaves and their families were at risk daily.

In that strange time after slavery and before true freedom

and equality, an elderly woman named Mary lived on the coast of North Carolina. She cherished her new-found freedom and moved herself and her son from Savannah to the Carolina coast. She had been given land there by her former master, and she understood that if she owned land, she and her son had a chance to reap some of the benefits of being free.

She was a seamstress and also did laundry for most of the white townspeople. Her wage wasn't much, only a few dollars a month, but it was enough for her and her son.

She kept a little garden in the back yard and grew almost everything they needed to eat. She went to town periodically for basics like flour, sugar, bread, and molasses.

Mary's son, Jessie, was her pride and joy. He was the only family she had left. Everyone else had passed on, so she clung to him and protected him in every way she could. She did everything she could to keep him with her.

Jessie grew up to be a fine-looking young man. Whenever Mary's friends came to visit, they'd remark about how handsome her son was.

Some of them even brought their daughters with them when they came. Many of them used visiting Mary as an excuse to introduce their daughters to Jessie. So Mary became very suspicious of people and stayed to herself much of the time.

Many of the young girls in the county had eyes for Jessie. He was not one to be impolite, so he treated them all with respect. Besides, he liked the attention he was getting and began to fancy himself as a dandy of sorts.

One young woman in the county was especially attracted to him. Her name was Sukey. Her every waking moment was consumed with thoughts of Jessie. Every day when she left the fields, she'd stop by Jessie's house. Sometimes she hid in the woods and waited until he came out. Just seeing him was enough for her.

After a time, she was bold enough to speak to him. And when he spoke back and was cordial to her, she took it as a sign that he liked her as well.

Although Jessie thought nothing of Sukey's infatuation, Mary was suspicious of her. "Jessie," she'd say, "don't spend too much time with that one. I don't like the way she looks at you."

"Oh, Ma," whined Jessie, "I can handle Sukey. She's harmless. She'd do anything I asked her to do."

"I just don't like her eyes, son. She needs so much love, and I don't think any one person can give her enough. People like that are very dangerous. They are just so starved for attention."

"All right, Ma. I'll watch it," said Jessie, half serious and half joking.

Time passed and Sukey became so jealous that whenever she saw Jessie talking to other girls she'd run them off.

Jessie became fed up and finally he confronted Sukey. "Girl, you don't own me! I can see who I please. You leave me be. I don't have no feelings for you, so just leave me be!" demanded Jessie.

Sukey was a strong girl and she didn't let much get to her, but when Jessie said that, she couldn't keep the tears back. She couldn't speak or face him, so she ran off.

Jessie said to himself, "I guess I told her! She won't be coming around here anymore!"

When Jessie went off to visit friends in town, it took him almost two hours to get back. Mary would let him travel to town only once a week, and that was usually on Sunday after they came from church, so he had to really high-tail it if he was going to get to town by early afternoon, spend a few hours there, and then get home before dark.

Mary always worried about him. She couldn't take a nap or even concentrate on her work until he returned safely.

One Sunday, night fell and Jessie still hadn't come home.

Mary waited for him to show two hours past his usual time, and then she decided to go looking for him. Not wanting to go alone, she went to a nearby widower's house and asked him if he would take her to town in his buggy.

The widower, Joe Smith, was glad to go anywhere with Mary. Since his wife had died, he had been all alone and had watched with great pleasure when Mary and Jessie moved into his rural community. Many times he had wanted to go by and visit, but he felt he should wait and take his time. He wanted to honor the memory of his first wife. A year had come and gone since she'd passed away, and now he was glad Mary had made the first move to communicate with him. Now he felt they could begin to be friends in earnest.

But he could tell this was not a good time for her. She seemed preoccupied, worried. When he talked to her, she didn't seem to be listening. It seemed as if her mind were someplace else. He even had to ask her questions more than once before she answered him. And she mumbled to herself as if she were scolding Jessie, even though he was nowhere around.

So he hooked up the mule to the wagon as quickly as he could and they started out.

She didn't talk much on the way into town, even though Joe tried to chat as they rode along. She'd just murmur, "Um huh," as if her mind were in other places. Whenever they encountered someone on the road, Mary would make Joe stop and ask if the person had seen Jessie. No one had.

Finally, after what seemed to Mary like forever, they arrived in the town of Creswell.

Jessie was a good boy and he always told Mary where he was going, so she knew his general whereabouts. Once she arrived in town, she decided to walk to a nearby creek where, he had told her, he liked to walk with his girlfriends. It was close enough to town so that someone was always passing by, but not so private that it would be indecent for a young lady and young gentleman to walk and talk privately.

Just as Joe and Mary rounded the bend in the path to the creek, she saw in the moonlight what looked like someone lying near the bank.

"What is that there, lying in the road?" asked Mary.

"I don't see anything," said Joe.

"Right there, up past that bend," said Mary.

Joe did see something this time. He told Mary to stay where she was and he would go have a closer look.

As he walked closer to the bend, he could clearly see that it was a person lying in the road, apparently unconscious. Looking closer, he now realized that it was Jessie. His body was still and there was blood under his head.

Almost as quickly as he realized it was Jessie, he started back toward Mary. She called to him, "What is it, Joe? What did you see?"

Finally reaching her, he replied as calmly as he could manage, "We got to get on out of here, Mary. We got to go and call the sheriff. Come on now. Let's go."

"Who is it? Who is it you saw?" asked Mary nervously. "Who is it?"

"Nobody. Now, let's go."

"You're lying. I can tell you're lying. I'm going to see for myself."

"No, Mary!" pleaded Joe. "Don't go over there! For God's sake, don't go over there."

But it was too late. She was on her way, and all his struggling with her did no good.

As she drew closer and closer to the body, she realized it was Jessie. "Jessie, boy, if you don't get up from there!" She reached down to shake him, as if he were asleep, and then she saw the blood under his head. She put both hands to her mouth. She began to bite her top lip and tremble uncontrollably. As she tried to steady herself, she tried again to convince herself that what she was seeing was not real.

"Jessie ... get up now. Jessie, Jessie get up." As if what she was seeing had finally registered in her mind, she let out a scream, "Jessieeeee ... Jessieeeeeeee ... Jessssssieeeeeee! Jesus ... Jesus ... what they done to my boy ... what they done. Jesus, oh my Jesus!"

They learned later from folks who had seen the couple that Sukey, in her anger and humiliation, had gotten into an argument with Jessie. They struggled, and Jessie fell and hit his head on a tree stump. He was killed instantly.

The sheriff didn't have any interest in investigating Jessie's death. In those days, there wasn't a great deal of concern for justice if a black girl killed a black boy. Whites didn't care, and they didn't see a need to rule the death anything other than an accident. After all, Jessie had a reputation for being a bit of a dandy, and this was just what happened when people like him got too full of themselves.

Besides, Sukey could do the work of two men, and most of the farmers in that area didn't see the logic of putting a prime field hand in jail just because of a silly accident, especially when she could be earning her keep.

Well, minutes turned into hours, hours to days, and days to weeks. And while Sukey didn't get any jail time, she did receive a great deal of punishment.

None of her family, or anyone else for that matter, wanted anything to do with her because of what she had done. It might have been an accident, but maybe it wasn't. Most of the people around her knew how obsessed Sukey was with Jessie, and so none of them doubted that it could have been something other than an accident.

If it hadn't been for Joe, it seems Mary would have just willed herself to death. She mourned Jessie day and night for almost twelve months. She and Joe spent most of their time together. Dinner, church, and nights when Mary had terrible nightmares, Joe was there to comfort her. Joe was the one who helped her recover from the deep depression in which she had lost herself. She had begun to get stronger, but there were still so many questions that she felt needed to be answered.

One day, as she and Joe were sitting on the porch, it came to her; she realized what she needed to do. She put down her sewing, stepped off the porch, and walked toward the fields she knew Sukey worked in.

"Where you going now, woman?" asked Joe.

"There's something I got to do, and I got to do it right now."

"Well, I'll come with you," offered Joe.

"No, Joe," she said with compassion. "This is something I must do by myself. I'll be back in a while."

Sukey was working in the fields as usual, and she paused to straighten up and give her back a rest. As she looked toward the edge of the field, she saw the figure of a woman coming toward her. As the woman came closer, she realized that it was Jessie's mama coming toward her.

Suddenly, Sukey was filled with anxiety. She and Mary had not spoken or even acknowledged each other since Jessie's death, and now here Mary was heading toward her. Sukey didn't know whether to go or stay.

As the other field hands looked up and saw Mary coming, they stopped working too. Sukey, paralyzed with fear, stood frozen in her tracks as Jessie's mother walked right up to her. Mary stared straight into her eyes and said, "You the one who killed my boy, ain't you?"

Sukey began to cry, fell to her knees, and said, "Yes, ma'am, yes, ma'am. I done it."

Jessie's mama looked down at her, helped her up, and said, "I can't cry no more, I can't grieve no more—no more tears left in me. You been grieving too, ain't you?"

"Oh yes, ma'am, oh yes. I never meant to hurt Jessie. I loved Jessie more than my own life. I just wish I hadn't gone to that creek that night."

"You come on and walk with me," said Mary. "I don't know how, but you and me got to make peace, or there ain't no hope for either one of us."

They walked off talking to each other that day. Folks say Mary and Sukey talked for the rest of that day and on into the night. Something must have happened that night, because from that point on, they were never out of each other's sight for any length of time. People say they were like mother and daughter. Many a night you could walk past Mary's place and see Sukey lying in Mary's lap as she hummed a tune and rubbed Sukey's weary brow.

We cannot see in the future.
We cannot see through the dark clouds.
We cannot see all the heartache.
Walk on, by faith, each day.

Joe and Mary lived with each other until they both passed on. Sukey took care of them both. When Mary died, she left all of her earthly belongings to Sukey. Years after Mary's death, you could pass by her place on any day and see Sukey sitting on the porch humming that song Mary always hummed for her.

Sukey passed away sometime after World War II, but folks say you can still pass by the old homeplace, and if you listen real carefully, you can hear Sukey humming still.

We cannot see in the future.
We cannot see through the dark clouds.
We cannot see all the heartache.
Walk on, by faith, each day.

STRUGGLE AND STRIFE

These stories focus on the process of moving toward freedom. Each story is about the successes, as well as, the failures that African Americans faced as they grappled with being free and black in white America. More importantly they are personal odysseys that illustrate the need we all have to be accepted, loved, and respected.

Much of the healing in the black community during the first years after the Civil War centered on blacks' negative images of themselves. Overcoming cruelly distorted self-images took time, patience, support, and love.

It didn't help that the South refused to accept the freedom of blacks, fighting it on every hand. Secret societies were formed such as the Ku Klux Klan, the Knights of the White Camellia, and the White Brotherhood. All sought to perpetrate systematic violence on blacks. These groups terrorized blacks and kept them from voting or seeking equality with whites on any level. Lynching, intimidation, beatings, and other violence escalated African Americans' fears, and many were scared to vote or express themselves in public.

In March 1865, the Bureau of Refugees, Freedmen and Abandoned Lands, the Freedmen's Bureau, was created. Its purpose was to offer food, supplies, and medical services, build schools, supervise contracts, and manage confiscated lands. By 1867, forty-six hospitals had been established to improve the health and sanitary conditions of thousands of freedmen. The bureau also started colleges such as Howard University and Storer College. When the bureau shut down in 1870, 247,330 students were attending 4,329 schools. But the crowning achievement of the

Reconstruction period was the passage of the Fourteenth and Fifteenth Amendments to the Constitution and the passage of the Reconstruction Act of 1867. These measures codified freedom and full citizenship for blacks.

Despite these advances, blacks throughout the South suffered socially and economically. In most cases, blacks could earn a living in the South in only three ways. One was to rent land from the white owner and farm it. This did not work well because whites did not want to surrender control of their land to blacks. Blacks could also work for wages. This was ineffective because in most instances whites refused to work with the Freedmen's Bureau, which was responsible for protecting former slaves' rights.

The third method, and most widespread, was sharecropping. Under this arrangement, the landowner provided tools, farm implements, draft animals, seeds, and the land on which to plant, cultivate, and harvest crops. Once harvest was over, blacks were to get a certain share of the money that came from selling crops. But this system manifested a major flaw. A line of credit was extended to freedmen and their families for goods that were provided by the landowner during the raising of the crops. This credit was extended until the harvest time, when blacks were expected to pay their debts. They were not to receive any profits until after their debts were paid. Extremely high prices for goods and interest rates charged by the white landowners left black farmers in so much debt that they found it almost impossible to make a profit.

The years between 1900 and 1950 saw a gradual decrease in lynchings and other violence toward blacks. Eventually, improved relations between blacks and whites began to change for the better. The two world wars also expanded opportunities for blacks. But the ultimate bid for equality started in the 1950s and culminated with the civil rights movement. ✳

Godmother

In 1974 I met a man in Detroit who, after hearing me tell a story to some teenagers on a street corner, decided to tell me one of his own. He told me that the only difference between what I did and what he did was that he told lies because the truth hurt too much. He told me his story, offered me a drink from his wine bottle, took a drink himself, shook my hand, and disappeared. I still regret that I didn't take the drink he'd offered.

❋ ❋ ❋

Once upon a time there was this fairy godmother who had three children, Calvin, Johnny, and Sadie. Calvin was sixteen, Johnny fourteen, and Sadie thirteen.

They didn't have a father—at least that's what Godmother always said. And for some reason, each time one of the children mentioned a father, Godmother would avoid talking about it. They were all pretty good children, and, for the most part, they treated Godmother with respect. She was a God-fearing woman and always told them to be good, responsible children, to eat the right foods, to make the right decisions, and to pick the right friends.

She was convinced that belief in God and daily prayer could deliver even the meanest sinner from a life of misery and suffering. She admonished her children to pray every day and to seek God in all they said and did.

It didn't take long for them to become tired of all the preaching and teaching of Godmother, so they began expressing themselves in other ways. They began doing things they shouldn't have.

Sadie discovered boys, and even though Godmother had talked to her about the "birds and the bees," Sadie became pregnant at the age of thirteen.

Johnny was the athletic type, always playing ball of some sort. And he was good at it, too. So good, in fact, that everyone thought he was the one who'd make it to a good life someday.

One night at a party, Johnny tried to show his friends how cool he was. He chug-a-lugged a fifth of scotch with two other friends. Feeling as if he were invincible, he went over to his girlfriend, who was talking with one of the neighborhood thugs, and accused the boy of trying to steal his girl. One comment led to another, and the thug invited Johnny outside to the parking lot. Johnny followed the young thug outside, and before he could lunge for the boy, he turned around and revealed a gun. Johnny backed off, but by then the commitment had been made and Johnny was shot. The bullet didn't kill him, but it did hit him in the kneecap. His leg had to be amputated, and his sports career was over.

Godmother worked at a hospital, cleaning up after the patients. Sometimes she worked into the evening, so she'd get home late at night. During work hours, however, she'd call her "little angels" to make sure they were all right.

Although they always said they were fine, they were far from it. The little angels were bored to tears and wanted to go out and be with their friends. So they took turns sneaking out and returning before Godmother came home from work.

Calvin was especially good at this, and since he was the oldest, it was natural that he should stay out the longest—at least that's what he told Johnny and Sadie. Being the oldest, everyone was supposed to look up to him, but it was Johnny everyone looked up to, including Calvin.

When Johnny lost his leg, it was proof positive for Calvin that they would always live in the projects. Johnny, with his ability in sports, was to have been their way out. Now there was no hope for them at all.

Godmother called twice a day during her breaks, at four o'clock to make sure they made it home from school and at 7:15 P.M. to make sure they were there and doing their homework. She was especially concerned about Sadie now and wanted to be sure she was eating and taking care of herself, especially with the baby coming.

Johnny's job was to look after Sadie, and he dedicated himself to that task as he had to his sports. He was like a brooding hen worrying over her chicks. And it seemed that Sadie even began to slow down a little and act more responsibly.

But Calvin was another story. He showed no concern for Sadie or Johnny now. The lessons they had learned the hard way were still not enough to convince him that he was also on the wrong path.

For Calvin, nothing was sacred. The little belief he had had in God he felt was now gone forever. He had prayed for Johnny often. He had prayed that Johnny would become famous so he could rescue them from a life of poverty and crime, but his prayers were not answered. So, he thought, why continue to pray? Why even continue to believe? Good fortune happened to others, not to him and his family.

In school, Calvin stole tests and cheated off papers with such skill that the teachers were convinced he should be in the gifted and talented program. Calvin had come to believe that there was as much to be learned from cheating and lying as there was in doing things the right way. He became a master at lying and deceit. Each victory emboldened him.

One day he decided he'd steal a bottle of wine from the corner store. The clerk in the store had seen him come in many times on errands for Godmother, so because Calvin was a regular customer, the clerk didn't watch him as closely as he did some others in the neighborhood.

Calvin pilfered the wine, put it under his jacket, walked up to the clerk, smiled, and asked how his day was going. He then put a Snickers bar on the counter, paid for it, and exited the store with the bottle of wine still in place under his jacket.

He found a quiet alley near his house, opened the bottle, and took a taste of wine for the first time in his life. It was good, and it made him feel good, too. Godmother had said nothing about wine tasting good. Well, how could anything so good be evil? He decided she was wrong.

He liked wine, so he found ways to get more and more. He lied to neighbors about Godmother forgetting to give him lunch money. He hit up the deacons from the church they attended. He even stole from Godmother. Once, he even convinced a janitor to give him money for a field trip that didn't exist.

Soon he began experimenting with hard liquors like rum, gin, and vodka. He liked rum the best.

It wasn't long before one of the gangs in the neighborhood began to notice Calvin. Maybe he wasn't the loser they had pegged him to be, so they let him hang out with them.

In no time he'd won them over. They liked him because he was funny as well as fearless. Nothing seemed to faze him. He was a natural gang member. They liked the way he walked and talked and acted, even though he did those things that way only when he was high on wine or liquor.

But no matter how good he was at hiding his drinking from his sister and brother, Godmother always knew better.

The night that she first caught him drinking in the bathroom, she put the strap to him so hard that it took Calvin's breath away. By now, however, he fancied himself to be a man, so he didn't let her know how badly it hurt. He paid her back for the punishment by stealing the cash she had set aside for paying the rent.

Calvin's behavior became worse and worse. Johnny and Sadie tried to talk to him, but he wouldn't listen to them. He'd convinced himself that they were losers as he once had been.

The gang was Calvin's new family. And in any case it was too late for him to pull out. He knew too much about them. They'd convinced Calvin that he was headed for better things—as long as he stayed with them. They also told him that his family only wanted him to be different because they were selfish and didn't want what was best for him. They told him that his mama wanted him to earn an honest living, but that when you were poor and black, the only thing you needed to learn was how to survive in jail. And since the white man had doomed all black people to failure, no matter what you did, you might as well have some fun and live large before they eventually caught you.

One day as Calvin was coming home from school, he saw an ambulance at his house. He'd reached the point where some mornings he'd go to school and some mornings he'd skip school and go hang with his gang. That morning he'd gone to school.

As he ran up to the house, he saw paramedics bringing out Sadie. They had this plastic thing over her mouth and nose. He ran in the house to see what had happened. The first person he saw was Godmother.

When she looked at him, it was as if she were sticking knives in his heart.

"Get out!" she yelled. "I never want to see you around my family again. If Sadie dies, I hope you die too."

Calvin tried to find out what was wrong, but no one would

talk to him. His brother simply walked away from him when he asked what had happened. He eventually found out his gang had harmed Sadie. Trying to save Calvin, she had gone to talk with the gang members.

Sadie had gone to the abandoned warehouse the gang called its pad. Although she knew this was a risky situation, she felt the danger was worthwhile if she could persuade them to leave Calvin alone. One of the gang members met her at the door of the dilapidated building. "What you want here, Mama?" he said.

"I want to talk to Vic. I hear he's leading you thugs."

"You're Calvin's sister, right?" asked the guard.

"Yeah, and I want to talk to Vic about my brother, unless you plan on writing a book about my visit," Sadie said.

"You keep it up with the smart mouth, and you won't be seeing anyone else today. You got it?"

"Yeah, I got it," Sadie said, backing off.

The gang member led her into a room in the back of the warehouse and told her to wait there. After a minute, three people entered the room, and she could tell immediately who was Vic. He had attitude, an air of self-confidence that was menacing. The other two gang members seemed frightened of Vic. They watched him intensely, waiting for a clue to how they should react. He thrived on the attention.

"Stay away from Calvin. Leave him alone," demanded Sadie.

Without warning, Vic pulled out a butcher knife and lunged at Sadie. "You'd better show me some respect, or you're a dead woman."

"Oh yeah? Well, you better stay away from my brother," she retorted.

Vic charged forward, too quickly for Sadie to react, and stabbed her several times. Without looking to see if she was dead or alive, Vic flicked his hand, motioning for the others to drag her out of his pad. He turned and walked away, and the gang members tossed Sadie into the street.

Sadie made it home, but she had lost a lot of blood. She managed to call the police, and they dispatched an ambulance from the hospital where Godmother worked. She rode home in the ambulance. She got home in time to see Sadie struggling with all her being to stay alive.

The gang had convinced themselves that Vic's actions wouldn't affect Calvin that much. After all, he was one of them and they had told him about families. Besides, he wasn't supposed to feel anything anyway, because he was always high. He surely would not feel any hostility or hatred for his gang family. After all, it was Sadie who had started it. He'd be drunk, as he always was, they said. He wouldn't even realize what had happened.

But he wasn't drunk. He had gone to school that day, and as a sober teenager he had witnessed his sister's death and his family's suffering.

But even if he had been drunk, he would have remembered. Being drunk makes you feel even more pain. You just think you care less. So Calvin had good reason to drink that day. He'd lost his gang, his sister, his mother, and his family, and none of them cared if he lived or died.

❋   ❋   ❋

Thirty-two years later, Calvin was still fighting the temptation to drown himself in booze. He was fifty years old and still haunted by the memory of Sadie's death and his family abandoning him.

Calvin spent a lot of time at the local YMCA and in Juvenile Hall. He tried to find young black boys who reminded him of himself, and he tried to help them avoid following his lifestyle. Some listened. Some didn't. Some he reached. Some, like him, could only learn from the truth of the streets.

But the street is a harsh teacher. "The streets may not allow you to make a mistake and learn from it," he often told them. "Any mistake, no matter how innocent, could end up being the last one made."

Calvin tried to tell them that. He tried to reach out as Godmother, Johnny, and Sadie had at a time in his life when they cared about him.

He didn't think family was important back then. In 1974 when I met him, he had learned the hard way that family is the only thing that is important.

The Lynching

The only case that I am aware of in which a black man was supposed to be lynched and lived to tell about it happened in Marion, Indiana, on August 6, 1930. One of my goals, as an African-American historian and storyteller, is to honor the historians of our past. When possible, instead of listening to what others say about us, I try to teach what African Americans said about themselves. In the case of James Cameron, we have a record that is vivid, descriptive, and harsh, but, based on my research, truthful. It is story about a brutal time told by a man who suffered beyond most of our capacities to understand such treatment. For that reason, it is an important story to hear, examine, and understand. Although I have adapted it to focus on the actual lynching, I have been faithful to his story in every aspect, paraphrasing instead of quoting the text in full.

* * *

Marion, Indiana, was a small midwestern town that in the 1920s and 1930s boasted a small population of blacks. Even though it was in the Midwest, it was home to the same prejudices as many southern towns. In 1930 the Ku Klux Klan held its annual state convention in Marion. Klansmen had plenty of power and were known for their ability to get certain people elected to state offices at will. They were organized and heavily armed with rifles, handguns, swords, and knives. They committed murders, arsons, bombings, and lynchings. They terrified witnesses and gained control of policemen, sheriffs, judges, juries, mayors, doctors, lawyers, and even the state legislature. Most of their crimes went unpunished.

But there was no race problem in Marion. The four thousand or so blacks who lived in the town mostly stayed on or near Western Avenue. They knew there were certain places they could and could not go. As long as they stayed in "their place," there was no problem.

Being a teenager anywhere means that most of the time you're bored with nothing to do. And it seems the only interesting things to do are those that are not allowed. Sixteen-year-old James Cameron, known to friends as Apples, was no different from any other teenager in the summer of 1930. On the night of August 6, 1930, Apples and two of his buddies, Tommy Shipp and Abe Smith, decided they wanted to cross some boundaries. Tommy, who had a 1926 Ford coupe, asked Cameron and Abe to go for a ride one night after he and a bunch of other boys from the neighborhood had gotten tired of pitching horseshoes.

While they were driving along, Abe said, "I want to hold up somebody tonight. I need me some money so I can buy me a new car."

Cameron became scared, but Tommy said, "Don't worry. There's nothing to it."

To prove how easy it was, Abe pulled a .38-caliber revolver out of his bib overalls. Abe said, "I'll be the leader. You two can be my gang!"

They stopped the car near a place in town called Lover's Lane at about nine o'clock. A mixture of fear, excitement, and confusion swirled in Cameron's mind as he followed Abe along the path into Lover's Lane.

They came to a car parked off the road in some bushes. A man and a woman sat in the back seat, and they were too busy talking to one another to notice the boys. Abe whispered to the other two, "We'll see how much money they got and then we'll take it."

Cameron whispered that he was afraid.

Abe said, "Look, all you have to do is throw the gun on people, and they'll stick up their hands. If they don't, you shoot them." Then he handed the gun to Cameron and said, "Here, Apples, you stick them up, and Tommy will search them."

Cameron told Abe, "I can't do it. Suppose the people in the car have a gun, too?"

Abe ignored him and shoved the gun into his hand. Cameron felt there was nothing he could do but go along with the plan. He walked up to the car, opened the door, and said, "Stick 'em up."

Abe then came out of the bushes with his right hand in his pocket as if he had a gun too. He said, "All right, come on out of the car and keep your hands up."

Cameron could tell Abe had done this before from the authority in his voice, and he seemed to know just what to do and say. The man and woman got out of the car with their hands high in the air.

Cameron didn't know the woman, but he immediately recognized the man. He regularly shined the man's shoes. He had a part-time job at the interurban railway station in town. Cameron remembered that the man always gave him good tips. He wouldn't let anybody shine his shoes but Cameron, no matter how long he had to wait. Because Cameron knew the man and the man had been so nice to him, it seemed to shake him into the realization that what he was doing was wrong. It seemed to convince him that he needed to get out of there. He handed the gun back to Abe and told him that he was going home. He then started to run as fast as he could. When he was about a quarter of a mile away, he heard the sound of gunfire. *Bang. Bang. Bang.* He ran faster after he heard the three shots. He ran as fast as he could until he reached his house.

It was well past ten o'clock, and his mother was waiting up for him as usual. She was sewing a patch on his overalls by the light of the kerosene lamp, which sat on a nearby end table. His mother never slept until all of her children were home safe.

"I wish you wouldn't stay out so late, James," she said to him as she opened the door to let him in. Then she got a good look at him and immediately knew something was wrong. He tried to hide his fear, but she knew, as she always did, that something was very wrong. "Look at your shirt," she said. "You're wringing wet with sweat."

"I've been playing football with some of the boys," he said. But she knew better.

"You're lying to me," she said. "Now tell me what it is. Are you in some kind of trouble?"

He wanted to break down and tell her everything. He wanted to lay his head in her lap and let her comfort him, but he was sixteen, her only boy, and he felt he would be letting her down if he told the truth. He was supposed to be the man of the house. With no father around, he felt he needed to be strong—or appear to be. "Aw, Mom," he said, "there's nothing wrong with me." Another lie.

"Go on upstairs and go to bed. I'll talk to you in the morning," she said.

Lying in his bed, all kinds of thoughts went through his mind. He tried to convince himself that he had done nothing wrong. But the scene kept creeping back into his mind. The one thing he had known since he was a little boy, the one taboo he had always kept straight in his mind, the one thing he had always understood was the danger of being in a white woman's presence. Don't look at them, don't go near them, and don't touch them, he remembered. It didn't matter whether it was innocent or not—stay away from them. He had broken a cardinal rule. He had held a gun on one, and the thought of that paralyzed him with fear.

Just then it seemed the entire house shook. He bolted upright in his bed. *Rap. Rap. Rap.* There it was again, a pounding at the door downstairs. Before he heard any voice, he knew who it was. He wanted to die right there. If he could have willed himself to death, he would have done it right then and there.

He heard his mother's mattress squeak as she rose to answer the door. He heard the voices of men as they rushed in. He heard the rumbling of their footsteps as they bolted upstairs. He heard them yelling at his mother. He heard her crying and calling to Jesus for strength. He felt the powerful beams of flashlights on his face and his body. "That's him!" someone said. They dragged him down the stairs and shoved him into the police car. He saw the tears in his mother's eyes and the confusion on his sisters' faces as the men drove him off, handcuffed in the back seat. He wondered if he would ever see his family again.

The men put him in a small cubicle and shone a big light in his face so that he couldn't see who was in the room, not even the man questioning him. They told him they would beat the truth out of him. They called him horrible names. They said that Abe and Tommy told them he was the ringleader. They told him he might as well make it easy on himself and confess. Everyone in the police station looked at him with deep hatred. The lone black policeman seemed to distance himself. He even offered to do the beating.

For three hours, they questioned him. They accused him of shooting the white man and raping the white woman. They told him the woman told them that he had raped her. One man questioned him while a room full of others watched. Cameron repeated, time after time, that he was not there when the shots were fired. He said he didn't know what happened after he ran away. He told them that both people were all right and had not been touched when he left.

At that moment, a huge fist exploded with the force of a baseball bat on the side of his head. The blow knocked him out of his chair. He saw feet converging on him. Now they were kicking him in his face, his stomach, his chest, his head—all over his body. He was pummeled so fiercely and with such force that he felt he would die before they stopped. Each kick seemed to send him into recurring streaks of unconsciousness.

Just when he felt he was actually dying, the sheriff said, "Hold it!" He then put a piece of paper on the desk, slammed Cameron into the chair, and ordered him to sign the paper. As he struggled through bruised eyes to read what he was signing—another lesson he had learned from his mother—he felt a blurring hand across his face. "I said sign it, not read it," the voice said. By now his pain was too great, his head too dizzy and confused, and his will too weak to resist them. He signed the paper. Later he would find out that it was a confession admitting that Abe had raped the woman and Tommy had shot the man.

The jail cell they put him in smelled of unwashed bodies, blood, and urine. He couldn't help but think about his mother. All those years of talks and stories about the dangers of an ill-spent youth, all those Sundays in church, all those times she stayed up, all those prayers he knew she sent on his behalf—this was how he repaid her. He was sick with shame and humiliation. She did not deserve to witness this day, and something told him it would get worse. He said his rosary, prayed for forgiveness, and tried to will his sore and weary body to sleep.

In the bullpen the next morning, he heard the other prisoners talking about him.

"If they don't kill him before he gits a trial, they'll tell all kinds of lies on him and git him 'lectrocuted."

"My boy Charles here will be a grandfather before they turn him loose."

Shortly after breakfast, the men began going to various corners of the cellblock, playing dirty hearts with an old deck of cards. After a little while, Cameron noticed that, one by one, the prisoners began to leave the game and head for the window. A crowd was gathering outside the jail. He went to the window and saw about a hundred white people in small groups talking to one another outside the courthouse. One of the inmates looked at Cameron and said, "They ain't up to no good, and ya' can believe that."

For the next three hours, the men around him halfheartedly played cards, stopping each time they heard a sound coming from downstairs. They were quiet. They were uncharacteristically quiet.

About three o'clock that afternoon, a black prisoner came to Cameron's cell and told him someone was at the door and wanted to talk to him. His heart jumped for joy. It's Mama, he thought to himself. Now he could tell her how sorry he was. Now he could fall on his knees and ask for forgiveness. She would make sure everything was all right, as she always did, and most of all she'd forgive him for all the trouble he'd caused her.

He bounded up the corridor of the cellblock to the door. But when he arrived, he saw, instead of his mother, two white men. One he recognized as the mayor. The other man was slender and had flaming red hair. A white handkerchief covered the lower half of his face. His eyes pierced with coldness. He looked at Cameron as if he could have killed him on the spot. Cameron knew this man hated him with all his being.

"Your name James Cameron?" the mayor asked.

"Yes, sir," Cameron answered.

"How old are you?"

"Sixteen, sir."

"Have you ever been in trouble before?"

"No, sir," Cameron said.

"Have you any brothers and sisters?"

"I've got two sisters, no brothers."

Then the masked man said to the mayor, "Let's get out of here," and they left. What did they want? Was the mayor a Klan member? Did they come just so they could identify him so they'd know who to hang later? Were they coming back? Where were Abe and Tommy? Did the two men go to see them, too, or were Abe and Tommy already dead? His stomach ached, and he felt hollow inside.

Twilight finally came, and with it larger crowds gathered outside the jail. Word had gotten back to the cell that the only black physician in town had been notified that three black youths would be lynched that night. They would be taken from the jail and killed by a mob. This act had been planned with precision, and the newspapers had even printed rumors about a lynch mob gathering in Marion. Some whites, as well as blacks, who heard about it had called the governor. No one, including the black doctor, was able to reach the governor.

Most of the black men in town had moved their families out of town for safekeeping. The majority of them stayed in nearby Weaver. Although rumor had it that the black men were arming themselves and would return to Marion to fight the mob, the majority of them stayed in Weaver, praying and singing hymns.

At about 5:30 in the evening, word came from a local reporter that the white man Tommy had shot was near death. The only black policeman had his gun taken away by his supervising officer and was ordered to direct traffic near the city limits, well away from the jail.

Cameron sat on the edge of his bunk and prayed, asking God for deliverance. Exhausted, he soon fell into a deep sleep. But as soon as his eyelids closed, he was awakened by a crashing sound and the tinkling of glass. All of the prisoners froze with fear.

"They're throwing rocks through the windows," one said.

"They're trying to break into the jail," said another.

Cameron sprang up from his bunk and rushed to the window. A huge mob had gathered. As far as he could see in any direction, thousands of people stood shouting obscenities and pointing at the jail. People had arrived from all over the state. A guard said there were at least ten thousand. They yelled. They shouted. They cursed. They threw rocks. Some had guns, others pistols, others high-powered rifles. No police even tried to take their weapons away. Some had torches; others carried ropes, bats, clubs, pick handles, crowbars.

As he stared out the window, Cameron saw some of the people from his own town and neighborhood. He saw customers whose shoes he had shined, boys and girls who went to his school, men who'd sold him bread, meat, and candy from their stores, neighbors whose lawns he had mowed and whose cars he had washed and polished. Then he heard their screams. "Bust the door down!" "Turn those black animals loose!" "Get those dang niggers out of here!" These were his neighbors, his friends saying these things.

The sheriff came out briefly to face the crowd and asked the people to leave. But they continued their shouting and shook their weapons at him. Feeling very small and outnumbered, he quickly closed the door and went back inside the jail. "We're going to hang every last one of them," the crowd yelled. Then the mob moved closer and closer to the jail.

They poured gasoline on the brick jail four times in an attempt to set the whole building on fire, but to no avail. They tried until they ran out of gas.

The sheriff and his men decided not to shoot into the crowd because of the women and children who were there. One of the leaders in the crowd yelled, "Get a sledgehammer!" Each time the big man with the hammer hit the door, the crowd roared its approval. After a while the man was too tired to continue, and another man took over until finally the bricks around the door gave way. The crowd roared. Inside the jail not one deputy or law officer raised a hand to stop the advancing crowd.

The mob first went after Tommy, dragging him outside. A horde of people immediately swarmed around him. In a matter of seconds, he was a bloody mess, but they kept mauling him just the same. Even as several men put the rope around his neck, they continued to beat him. Finally they dragged his body around to the east side of the jail out of sight. They looped the rope through the bars of the first-floor window and hanged him there for all to see. For all of twenty minutes the throng pushed and shoved to get a close look at the "dead nigger." But they wanted more. "All right, Abe Smith. You're next," one of the leaders yelled.

They dragged Abe out and beat him so badly that he was dead before they hanged him. They hanged him on a tree on the courthouse lawn. Then they went back to the jail, got Tommy's body, and suspended him beside Abe.

After about fifteen minutes of celebrating, the leaders started back for Cameron. The crown began to chant, "We want Cameron! We want Cameron!" When the men reached his cell, none of the other prisoners would point Cameron out. When they asked Cameron if he was the one they were after, he denied it. The leader said, "Tell us which one is Cameron, or we are going to hang every one of you niggers." The prisoners pleaded. They crawled. They kissed the feet of the white men holding sway over them. Like trained animals, they humiliated themselves, begging the white men to spare their lives. Finally, one of the prisoners pointed Cameron out.

As they dragged him out, hands seemed to hold him like

vises. Fists, clubs, bricks, and rocks hit him on the face, arms—all over his body. He sagged lifelessly but did not pass out. Those who couldn't reach him spat at him. Little children bit and scratched him. They mauled him all the way to the tree on the courthouse lawn. Not once did they stop pounding on him. They put the rope over his head and swung the other end over the tree. He mumbled, half conscious, "Have mercy on me, Lord." He couldn't help but think of Jesus hanging between the two thieves and remember what his mama said about Jesus dying for his sins.

Then something strange and miraculous happened! Out of the crowd he heard a voice, unlike any other voice he had ever heard, say, "Take this boy back. He had nothing to do with any raping or killing!"

As if someone had snatched their voices, a mysterious silence settled over the mob. No one moved or spoke. It was as if everyone were hypnotized. All of a sudden Cameron felt hands that had been sinister and violent now removing the rope from around his neck with care and tenderness. He felt himself under the tree alone; the mob had drawn back. Heads were bowed. A path had opened from the tree to the steps of the county jail. Slowly he limped back to the jail. No one touched him. No one called him names. They all looked down, not allowing their eyes to meet his as he walked by. He was alive. He had escaped a horrible fate, an escape that no one thought possible. For some inexplicable reason, he had been spared.

James Cameron was sent to the Indiana State Reformatory, where he spent five years. He became a very religious man, and to this day, he believes that he was saved from his horrible fate by a miracle of God.

Liza Jane

We have all, at one time or another, looked at those around us and labeled them according to our own standards of beauty. We assign names to those who don't meet our standards: Tubby, Lardo, Beanpole, Skinny Minny, Stumpy, High Yellow, Chocolate, Buckwheat, Nerd, Bamma, Borilla. The list goes on and on. But, as Don Juan reminds us, the secret is in finding the beauty that lies just beneath the surface and honoring it. This is a story of a girl who thought she was ugly but found out that she possessed matchless beauty.

* * *

Liza Jane, Liza Jane,
somebody hit her with a frying pan.
She's too fat, face too black,
somebody hit her with a baseball bat.

She was born Elizabeth Jane Palmer, but before she reached the age of five, everyone in the neighborhood called her Liza Jane. She lived on the east side of Williamsburg, Virginia, near the College of William and Mary.

Her mother worked as a maid in one of the many motels around Williamsburg. Many of the motels had colonial names like The Captain John Inn, Pocahontas Motor Lodge, The Raleigh

Tavern, The Carriage Inn, and The Patrick Henry Inn.

There were streets like Duke of Gloucester, England, Scotland, South Henry, Queen's Creek, Jamestown Road, York Street. Communities were named York Terrace, James Terrace, Queen's Lake, where all the rich people lived. And then there were names like Iron Bound and Grove, Highland Park, Centerville, Carter's Neck, Lightfoot, and Toano, where most of the blacks in town lived.

Liza lived in one of those communities. Like most little girls in her neighborhood, she played with dolls, rode tricycles, played hide-and-seek, and rejoiced when the Best Ever ice cream truck rolled through her neighborhood.

She was the apple of her daddy's eye, and she fought with and tattled on her two brothers and sisters just as other kids did.

In fact, she never thought of herself as being different until she entered the sixth grade. That was when girls began to change. They began to grow and develop. They were becoming young women. Most sixth-grade girls began to pay close attention to how they looked, what they wore, and what others thought of them.

Boys, too, began to look different. Girls realized that boys were no longer just friends to play baseball with or throw rocks at when they made them mad. They noticed that some of them were even cute. Some of them even made the girls feel funny when they were around them. Girls longed for boys to smile at them, notice what they were wearing, or just spend time talking to them. And so did the boys.

Everyone who lived in Liza's neighborhood attended the same elementary school, but when Liza started the sixth grade, she had to go to another school. This school was farther away and much larger than her old school, with lots more kids.

When Liza arrived at her new school for the first time, many of these new kids weren't nice—especially to her. The girls didn't smile at her, and the boys laughed when they saw her. Some of them even refused to sit by her in class. They made faces when she walked down the halls. They pointed at her in the lunch room and called her names, names that made fun of her face, her hair, her clothes, and her speech.

> *Liza Jane, Liza Jane,*
> *she so ugly it's a cryin' shame.*
> *Face so fat, face so black,*
> *somebody hit her with a baseball bat.*

Instead of the neighborhood kids standing up for her, they seemed more interested in making friends with the very people who gave Liza trouble.

At first Liza cried when they taunted her, but after a while she became angry and retaliated. After a while, she began to chase the kids who insulted her and said cruel things. She'd catch them and wrestle them to the ground and take out her frustration on them. She'd try to make their faces look just like they said hers looked.

But the fighting just got her into more trouble. She was suspended twice and almost expelled before the school year was out. She ended the school year depressed, humiliated, and ostracized.

She was trapped. She couldn't go to another school, and she hated the school she was in.

That summer, Liza was to have an experience that would change her life. Her parents sent her to West Virginia to visit her Aunt Sadie, who had lived in the same hills all her life. Although Liza knew her Aunt Sadie, this was the first time she had visited her.

Aunt Sadie was famous in Liza's family. Throughout her life, Liza had heard all kinds of stories from her cousins about Aunt

Sadie and how strange she was. She had no husband, had never been married, and lived alone in a haunted house. She kept a black snake for a pet. Aunt Sadie possessed eyes that could hypnotize a person.

Liza's cousins said Aunt Sadie came out only at night, and she would roam for hours in the pitch black. About sunup she'd come back talking to herself. Some of the cousins even claimed Aunt Sadie knew voodoo and hoodoo, and that's why she was going out at night, to commune with the spirits.

Her mother told her it was all nonsense, that Aunt Sadie was very self-sufficient but that was all. She did everything herself. She cooked, cleaned, tended the garden, repaired her old house, and could even fix the old car she drove, all by herself. It was true she never married, but that was her choice, not her fate, Liza's mother told her.

Even so, Liza was not happy about spending time with Aunt Sadie at her place.

Liza remembered her father saying that Sadie believed men weren't worth the trouble it took to live with them. Liza never quite understood that, but the way those stupid boys had treated her in school, she could sure understand why she didn't want to marry one.

Aunt Sadie did seem nice, despite what her cousins said. Every Christmas and Easter, Aunt Sadie sent Liza a special gift. No one else in Liza's family received anything, but Liza always did.

Her mother said that when she first had Liza, she lived with Aunt Sadie while Daddy was trying to find work. As a baby, Liza was quite fond of Aunt Sadie. In fact, she would go to sleep only when Sadie rocked her or took her for a walk.

Aunt Sadie felt that Liza was special and had been from the day she was born. Sadie knew that Liza had to believe she was special too, or she would be doomed to always judge herself by the standards of others.

Liza arrived in the little town of Elkins, West Virginia, early on a Monday morning. The summer sun stifled what air there was, and the humidity made Liza feel sticky. She sat on a bench outside the small bus station, wishing her Aunt Sadie would come quickly and hoping she had air conditioning in her car and house.

In a few short minutes, Sadie arrived in a car that looked as old as she was. When Aunt Sadie stepped out of the car, what Liza saw made her want to get back on the bus.

Aunt Sadie was dressed in a pair of coveralls that were way too long for her, so she had to roll them up at the cuffs. She had on big brogan boots and an old straw hat with a snakeskin band circling it. A clay pipe dangled from her mouth.

Her face was as rough as the back of an alligator, and her eyes were as black as the night, eyes that looked dead and motionless. Liza's cousins were right. Those eyes did have the power to hypnotize.

But there was something else about her eyes that her cousins hadn't mentioned. When Aunt Sadie looked at Liza, it was as if she were looking through her, as if she could understand what Liza was thinking. It was creepy, thought Liza, but it was also strangely comforting.

As they drove to Aunt Sadie's house, Liza hardly said a word, and neither did Aunt Sadie. It was as if she knew that Liza needed time to get used to her. She didn't push Liza to say anything. She seemed to instinctively know what Liza needed. She just silently drove along. Every so often, she'd tap that clay pipe with her index finger. The burning tobacco didn't even singe her finger!

Even though Aunt Sadie was strange, Liza never felt that she was in harm's way when she was around her. In fact, the more Liza was around Aunt Sadie, the more she felt safer.

Aunt Sadie's house was a four-room cabin that sat on top of

a large mountain. It had no running water and no television. The only good thing about the house was that it overlooked a beautiful field at the front and a wonderful mountain ledge at the back. When they arrived, Liza caught sight of two of Sadie's pets. She had a three-legged dog and a tabby cat, and both ran toward the car as they drove up.

The dog seemed glad to see Liza, and it came up to her almost immediately. Liza began talking to the dog and playing with it. Aunt Sadie took her bags from the car and smiled approvingly.

After putting her bags down, Aunt Sadie returned outside to find Liza still playing with the dog. In a soft but powerful voice, she commanded, "Get away there, Dandy." The dog stopped in his tracks, backed up, and slithered away under the house.

"We ain't got time to play now, Liza. Come on in the house and set at the kitchen table." Liza walked inside the house. It was small but at the same time very comfortable.

The middle of the room had a big stone fireplace with logs stacked up beside it. A dried gourd and a picture of Liza with her mother, father, brothers, and sisters sat on the mantle. To the right of the front door was a small kitchen area with a stove, a refrigerator, which Aunt Sadie called an icebox, a hot water tank, a counter top, and cabinets with no doors. She had three chairs at the kitchen table, all different in style, color, and material. One was all wood, one had a cane seat, and cloth covered the third. Liza sat on the cloth one; it was softer on the behind. She sat quietly as Aunt Sadie began to speak. "I brought you out here for one reason and one reason only. I know you don't like being here, and I know you and the rest of your family think I'm touched in the head. That don't bother me none. But here's what does bother me—you doing poorly in school. Don't you know if you don't do good in school you'll wind up being nothing? Education is power; *no* education is just plain slavery. What's wrong with you, girl? Why you getting in so much trouble?"

"Nothing is wrong with me," said Liza.

"Nothing is what got you chasin' Johnny Robinson in the woods and beating up on him?" asked Sadie knowingly.

"How you know about that?" Liza asked, puzzled.

"There ain't too much I don't know about you, girl. You and me is connected." Then as quickly as Sadie had begun her conversation, she ended it and walked away from Liza.

That night as they ate supper, Sadie said, "I want you to take this smooth rock I've got for you. It's a magic rock. Put some of my roots on it. Whenever someone says something mean to you, look at them, rub the rock and say, 'I like you just the same.' That rock will change their hearts, and they will change the way they treat you from the time you rub this rock until the day they die."

Liza didn't question her Aunt Sadie. If she said that rock was magic, then Liza was more than willing to believe it was.

The week with Aunt Sadie went by very fast, and Liza had a better time than she had thought she would. She spent hours on end lying in a bed of lilacs or blowing dandelions all around and watching them float in the wind. It was good not to have her brothers and sisters to worry about, or having to listen to those mean-spirited children at her school.

Up on that mountain with Aunt Sadie, she felt as if she were the most beautiful girl in the world, and nobody told her differently.

And now that she had the magic rock, she was sure that nobody would make fun of her ever again. She smiled to herself as she practiced saying the magic words and rubbing the rock. "*I like you just the same.*"

Finally the day came for Liza to leave. She looked so peaceful, confident, and rested. The week with Aunt Sadie was just what she needed, she told herself. In fact, it was downright fun. Aunt

Sadie treated her with respect and cared about her feelings, and that made it extra nice. So Liza returned home from her trip refreshed and eager to try out her magic rock.

As soon as she was settled and unpacked, she rode her bike to the playground on the east side of town. She knew most of her enemies from school would be there. She spotted old Jasper Mitchell right away. He was the ringleader of the group that was always giving her trouble. When Jasper saw her, he began to laugh and started to say something mean to her.

Quick as a flash, she took the rock from her pocket and began to rub it. Then she said the magic words, "I like you just the same." Jasper fell silent, looked at Liza, and smiled—he actually smiled at her—and then he asked her if she wanted to play ball with them.

Hot dog, Liza thought to herself, *it works!*

She played baseball for the rest of the afternoon and got three hits too.

As the week progressed, each time someone saw Liza and tried to make fun of her, she'd take out the rock and say the magic words. It worked every time. Liza was beside herself with joy.

And then something strange happened: Liza began to change. She walked differently and she began to dress in different ways. She talked in softer tones and with greater confidence. Liza started treating others nicely, and they, in turn, treated her the same.

As the days passed, Liza began to realize that she didn't even need the rock for people to treat her with respect. She commanded respect simply by the way she treated others and the way she began to carry herself with confidence and pride.

Soon, Liza didn't need the rock at all. And what was even more exciting, she was doing very well in her schoolwork. When her interim grades came out, they were the best she had made since coming to the school.

On Sunday, when telephone rates were lowest, Liza's mother let her call her Aunt Sadie to let her know about her progress. She told her about the rock and how she believed in its magic at first. Liza also told her that she didn't even need the rock anymore. Liza told Aunt Sadie about the improved grades and how her mother and father were so proud of her progress. But, of course, Aunt Sadie already knew.

"I ain't surprised," said Aunt Sadie over the phone. "You never needed it in the first place. I never put no spell on that rock. It was just a rock I found in the road the day I picked you up from the bus station.

"Girl, if you don't think you're worth beans, nobody else will either. If you want people to think you're beautiful, you got to think it first. If you want people to treat you nice, you got to be nice first. You were never ugly. You are the most beautiful girl in the world, but your beauty starts inside yourself. Once you realize that, then everybody else sees it too. I got to go now. You comin' to see me next summer?"

"Yes ma'am, I sure am," said Liza. "Aunt Sadie?"

"What is it, child?"

"How come you so smart and all?" asked Liza.

"I just believe that I am, and that's all there is to it. If I believes it, then I start doing things smart people do, like reading books and listening more than I talk and seeing things for what they really are, and not so much for what I can really see with my eyes. All you got to do is wish it. And if you have faith in yourself and the goodness of God, you can do and be anything you want to. Now get off this phone 'fore your mother has to pay a big phone bill. I've been thinkin' hard on that one, but I ain't come up with a spell to make these phone calls free." Aunt Sadie giggled.

"Bye, Aunt Sadie," said Liza. "I love you."

"Bye, child. I love you too, you pretty thing you!"

THE JOURNEY CONTINUES ...

On December 1, 1955, Rosa Parks, a black seamstress living in Montgomery, Alabama, quietly entered the chronicles of history. Weary from her day's work, she boarded a city bus and sat in the first empty seat she saw. The seat was in the front of the bus. Jim Crow laws in the South required blacks to sit in the back of the buses, with whites in the front. When a white man got on the bus and the only available seat was the one occupied by Parks, the bus driver stopped the bus and asked her to move to the rear. Parks refused to move and was arrested. Her action led to the Montgomery Bus Boycott and started a chain of events that sparked the historic civil rights movement.

A young black preacher who had just received his doctoral degree from Boston University's School of Theology, Martin Luther King, Jr., was asked to lead a protest against the Montgomery bus system, and, as a result, blacks refused to ride city buses for three hundred and eighty-one days. The boycott resulted in the city acquiescing and integrating the bus system and also hiring black bus drivers.

The civil rights movement also brought about a new energy and spirit within the African-American community. Many apathetic voices had found the spark they needed to speak out. King eventually helped form the Southern Christian Leadership Conference. However, black leadership suffered great losses during the period. King, Malcolm X, and Medgar Evers were killed; Whitney Young died; H. Rap Brown was jailed; Stokely Carmichael and Eldridge

Cleaver had to live in exile. But on what looked to be the sunset of the civil rights movement, new voices emerged: Imamu Baraka, Jesse Jackson, Coretta Scott King, Roy Innie, Vernon E. Jordan, John Lewis, and Julian Bond were beginning to emerge, stressing the importance of understanding the black experience in its totality.

Inequities remain today. For example, nowhere in America is the median family income for African Americans equal to that of whites. The infant mortality rate is twice that of the white population, the health of African Americans appears to be decreasing, and African Americans still have the highest mortality rate of any ethnic group in the United States.

These stories relate to my family and me as I grew up in Williamsburg, Virginia, during the turbulent 1960s.

Daddy and the Black Barnstormers

This is a story about a little-known community of black aviators who were instrumental in helping African Americans enter the field of aviation. Through their tenacity, courage, and determination, they helped desegregate the armed forces of the United States. They also were responsible for the pilot training programs that began in 1941 in such places as Hampton Institute in Hampton, Virginia, and Tuskegee Institute in Tuskegee, Alabama. The most famous of these aviators were the Tuskegee Airmen, who distinguished themselves during World War II.

I became interested in this aspect of aviation history during a storytelling session that I attended at the Smithsonian Institution in Washington, D.C., when a curator from the National Air and Space Museum joined with a fine storyteller, Syd Lieberman, who told a story about aviation that was wonderful, sad, poignant, inspiring, and, most importantly, educational. But he didn't talk much about black aviators, and I wondered why.

The story also made me think of my dad. He loved flying. For eleven years, he worked hard to learn to fly and obtain his pilot's license. I still have vivid memories of the journey he took to get his commercial pilot's license.

I didn't think my dad was alone in his interest, but I didn't know for sure. It was Syd's story that piqued my curiosity about the history of African Americans in aviation, and whether or not my dad's experience was indeed unique.

So I did a little research and found that my dad was not alone in his love of flight; many others had come before him. Their stories are fascinating and inspiring. In honor of those African-American pilots and of my dad, Floyd T. Ellis, who shared their love for the skies, I offer this story.

✹ ✹ ✹

I was raised in Williamsburg, Virginia. When I was about eight or nine years old, my father, who was a brick mason, contracted a fever. The condition was not unknown to black people during that time, but it was a rare fever that lasted quite awhile—at least eleven years. Every Sunday he dragged the family to a spot on the outskirts of the town, and we sat patiently in a parking lot waiting for him.

My dad wanted to fly. My sister, my brother, and I watched in awe as he took off in his Piper Cub or his rented Beechcraft to float in the air for an hour or so. Sometimes, as he touched down and soared back up, he would flap his rudders to wave at us.

In my town my dad was lower-middle class, uneducated by the standards of those times, and a laborer. No one expected him to fly. None of my friend's fathers or any other blacks in the town ever attempted flying, but my father did, and I was proud of him.

Our family went to all the air shows in the area, and I stood dumfounded as pilots performed loop-the-loops, flew upside down, stood on the wings of planes, and parachuted from the air as if the tricks were as simple as tying shoelaces. But for me, the real hero was my dad. He may not have been able to fly in the air shows, because of his race, but he did fly. From 1955 to 1966, he gave it his best shot. I didn't learn until I was grown why he never got his commercial pilot's license. I didn't know that discrimination, segregation, and lack of money had driven him from something he loved.

I took the time, however, to find out the reason, and I'm glad I did. I learned a lot about my dad. But I also learned a lot about African Americans and their role in aviation history.

✹ ✹ ✹

It all began on a cold December morning in 1903 in Kitty Hawk, North Carolina, when two young bicycle mechanics transformed a dream, a dream shared with the likes of Leonardo da Vinci, into a reality. On December 17, they achieved the first sustained powered flight, and the world would never be the same.

It would be at least twenty years after that historic flight before the first African American achieved the dream of flight. But this was only sixty-one years after the end of slavery and barely one generation from the time when blacks were still being lynched, denied equal education, and belittled in minstrel shows throughout the nation.

African Americans began to break into aviation during the decade after Charles Lindbergh made the first nonstop solo flight over the Atlantic in 1927. It was as if they too looked up at the stars and said, "I want to do that."

Richard Wright's 1940 novel, *Native Son,* describes two black boys watching in awe and frustration as an airplane performs intricate skywriting maneuvers above them. "I could fly a plane if I had a chance," says one to the other. The other remarks, "If you wasn't black and if you had some money and if they'd let you go to that aviation school, you could fly a plane."

The evolution of the automobile engine gave the development of airplanes a huge boost. And the 1920s and 1930s became known as the golden age of flight.

African Americans wanted to fly too. But segregation in

America insinuated that blacks simply lacked the intelligence to fly. They couldn't get into aviation schools, no one would teach them to fly, and the military was also closed to them. African Americans, however, wanted to fly so badly that they accomplished extraordinary things with outdated and neglected equipment to prove their worth.

The airplanes in those days were flimsy to begin with, but these intrepid souls stepped inside machines constructed of fabric and wood and powered by motorcycle engines. They had to navigate by dead reckoning, or using landmarks as guides. Sometimes the vibrations were so great that parts of the plane flew off. Sometimes the weather was so cold the pilots could barely survive just a few minutes in the air.

When World War I began in 1914, the airplane had been around for only ten years. Planes were primitive. They were made of hardwood with fabric coverings and braced with wires. The cockpits were open to the elements. Some planes were so dilapidated they fell apart in the air. Most planes had no brakes. To slow a plane down for landing, a pilot had to kill the engine, and then hope that it could be restarted. When they did start the engines, the pilots stood only three or four feet from an unmuffled motor; it produced one hundred and twenty-five decibels of sound, and, with the propellers whirling, the noise increased another one hundred twenty decibels. For comparison, a pneumatic jackhammer produces just one hundred and ten decibels. Planes back then took off from a field, pasture, or meadow.

While flying, pilots often became nauseated from the castor oil used as an engine lubricant. In the air, pilots faced gale force winds in the open cockpits. Pilots said the air was so cold it was like breathing ice. If the temperature was sixty degrees on the ground, at twenty thousand feet it was forty-five degrees below zero. They also had to contend with a lack of oxygen at high altitudes. Pilots returning from flying often complained of sleepiness, a loss of concentration, and a feeling of drunkenness, but they had no idea what was causing these symptoms.

The absence of pressurized cabins also caused problems for fliers. If a pilot's blood pressure was one hundred and twenty at ground level, at six thousand feet it was two hundred. The pressure was so great pilots complained that the fillings in their teeth throbbed. They also reported that their helmets felt like vise grips. They suffered excruciating headaches, and descending from the sky too fast was like rising from the ocean floor. The oxygen rushing into the bloodstream and the increased circulation produced intense headaches and muscle spasms. Some pilots had to be carried from their planes when they landed. And during the war they weren't just flying, they were killing and being killed.

Yet all of this didn't stop those African Americans who wanted to soar.

Eugene Ballard was one such man. One of the first African Americans to receive a pilot's license, Bullard didn't let his race deter him. His own country's air force wouldn't give him a chance to fly, so he journeyed to France and fought for that country on the western front during World War I in a plane he named *All Blood Runs Red*. Bullard, a native of Columbus, Georgia, earned several awards, including the French La Croix de Guerre for his achievement in combat.

Another African-American pioneer in aviation, Bessie Coleman, achieved two important firsts. Not only was Coleman the first licensed African-American pilot, she was the first United States woman to earn an international pilot's license. She accomplished this in 1921, a time when many women viewed flying as a man's activity.

Not only race, but also gender, was a major stumbling block in the young aviator's life. But Coleman didn't let any of it stop her.

She learned French, left the United States with financial help from Robert Abbot, an African-American newspaper publisher, and took flying lessons in Europe.

Coleman dared to perform aerobatics that most male pilots feared. In June 1922, at Staaken Airfield near Berlin, she flew the largest plane ever piloted by a woman. In August of that same year, she returned to the United States with her pilot's license after having worked with a Red Cross unit attached to a French flying squadron in 1921.

In 1926 while she was practicing for an air show, Coleman's controls locked up. Tragically, she wasn't wearing her seat belt when the plane she was a passenger in spun out of control and turned over. According to Doris L. Rich in her book *Queen Bess: Daredevil Aviator*, "Eyewitness accounts of the altitude to which the plane descended varied but aviators who were watching said it went into a tailspin at 1,000 feet, then flipped upside-down at 500 feet. Bessie fell out, somersaulting end over end until she hit the ground with a sickening thud, crushing nearly every bone in her body...."

At the end of the twenties, William Powell organized the Bessie Coleman Aeroclub in Los Angeles. Born in Henderson, Kentucky, in 1897, Powell had been bitten by the aviation bug while attending a reunion in France.

His sister, Edna Gayle, remembered the trials he endured in Chicago while trying to obtain his license. "He went to the military school and tried to enroll in aviation, and the major told him, 'Oh, you could never fly a plane. You could never get in.' "

Powell asked him why, and the major said, "Because you have to have certain credentials. Just because you're an ex-soldier doesn't mean you can get in. You're supposed to have certain credentials."

Powell asked what the credentials were. The major explained that first one had to be a graduate of a university, and second one had to be an engineer.

Edna Gayle said, "So my brother picked the things the man said he needed out of the envelope he had brought with him. He showed him his sheepskin, and then his diploma in electrical engineering and showed him his certificate in foreign languages and romance languages. The man looked at him and almost cried. And then the man said, 'I'm sorry. I can't take you because you're a Negro. But I tell you what I will do, maybe you can come here when there's nobody here and I can teach you to fly.' And my brother said, 'That's what they told me when I went into the army to fight. No, I don't want it.' That was the first time I saw my brother cry."

But Powell didn't stop there. He found an aviation school in Los Angeles that accepted him. Finally, he was able to realize his dream. Powell hoped that aviation jobs would help unemployed blacks find work. His dream was to form one hundred aeroclubs in different cities, but it was not to be. He could not get enough sponsorship, money, or interest from the African-American or white communities.

Powell desperately wanted black youngsters to take up flying. He realized flying was an opportunity for African Americans' to gain equality in America. For him aviation, and African-Americans involvement in it, was more than a list of firsts for the history books. Powell believed that for every African-American pilot in the air an improvement in race relations would take place on the ground. He believed that flight was a vehicle for positive social change.

In August 1931, the first African-American air show was held in Los Angeles. It was so successful that Los Angeles city officials asked that another one be held in December to benefit the city's unemployment fund. Powell's dream had become a reality. People were paying attention to African Americans and their flying.

Like William Powell, James Banning, a native of Oklahoma, was an engineering student. He also ran an auto repair shop in Ames, Iowa. He was taught to fly by a World War I veteran. In an interview with the *Pittsburgh Courier*, Banning talked about training during winter blizzards. "I would shiver and shake through a half hour of student instruction. The cold weather gave my natural shivering instincts quite an outlet. I need not mention the added shivers provided by the shaking, trembling, dilapidated old plane in which we trained." Banning became the first black pilot licensed in the United States. He accumulated more than seven hundred fifty hours of flying time, which also made him eligible for a transport pilot's rating.

Powell and Banning knew and respected each other. They both wanted to set records in flying. They both dreamed big dreams and saw some of them become reality.

Banning purchased a used XX-6 Eagle Rock and along with Thomas Allen, a top-notch mechanic, set out to attempt a flight across the continent. But because of racial barriers, Banning couldn't find financial support. That didn't stop him. On September 18, 1932, he and Allen, calling themselves the Flying Hobos, left Los Angeles in the World War I plane with a fourteen-year-old engine and less than one hundred dollars for gasoline and oil. Banning had decided before leaving to fly a southern route instead of a midwestern one. The pair stopped in black sections of towns and visited houses where African Americans, who were eager to support their efforts in any way, fed and housed them for free. As they inched their way toward New York, the Flying Hobos became heroes and received coverage in both black and white newspapers.

On the Sunday morning of October 9, 1932, the Eagle Rock landed in Roosevelt Field on Long Island, three weeks after its departure from Los Angeles. The Flying Hobos had accumulated a total flying time of forty-one hours and twenty-seven minutes.

New York Mayor Jimmy Walker gave them the key to the city, and Cab Calloway and Duke Ellington wined and dined the aviators in Harlem. They returned to Los Angeles, and Banning continued his role as the chief pilot for the Bessie Coleman Aeroclub.

On February 5, 1933, Banning, at age thirty-two, was flying as a passenger in a biplane being flown by a white pilot. The pilot didn't have Banning's experience, yet he insisted on flying the plane. The plane crashed, and both men were killed. One reporter said, "Banning had joined Bessie Coleman in that Valhalla of Death, reserved for those gallant souls who have the courage to face even death in an unequal struggle with their equipment and race prejudice. They proved that Negro boys and girls could indeed fly."

In 1933 and again in 1934, C. Alfred Anderson and Dr. Albert E. Forsythe flew from Atlantic City, New Jersey, to Los Angeles to become the first African Americans to fly a round-trip transcontinental flight. In 1934, they also flew a Pan-American goodwill flight in a plane they christened the *Spirit of Booker T. Washington*. The president of Tuskegee Institute, the noted educator Robert R. Moton, was a supporter, along with the National Urban League. Both men hoped that their flights would inspire black youth to see aviation as an avenue for advancement.

The struggle continued. Pilots in the Challengers Air Pilots Association—Johnny Robinson, Harold Heard, and Cornelius Coffey—continued in the tradition of Banning and Coleman in promoting aviation in the African-American community. They even tried to persuade Tuskegee to begin an aviation program long before World War II began.

Ironically, the Chicago-based Challengers Air Pilots Association, which was started by Cornelius Coffey, and the Los Angeles-based Bessie Coleman Aeroclub were involved in the same flying activities at the same time but did not know about each other.

Hubert Julian, known as the Black Eagle, was the flamboyant flier who united the two aeroclubs. Julian gained fame as the black pilot who supported Marcus Garvey's Negro Improvement Association, a "militant" black organization dedicated to black nationalism. Many pilots were upset with Julian because they thought his popularity as an aviator was greater than his ability. Although he was an extraordinary self-promoter, he made more promises than he kept.

By the end of the 1930s, the United States began noticing the incredible flying abilities of African Americans, something European countries had recognized all along. In 1939, the federal government provided an impetus for change when Congress established the Civilian Pilot Training Program, which gave blacks their first opportunity to participate in federally funded flight training programs.

After the attack on Pearl Harbor, which brought the United States into World War II, the Civilian Pilot Training Program became the War Training Service Program. This program also supported training for African Americans at six black colleges in the eastern United States and two non-academic flying schools in the Midwest, including Tuskegee Institute in Alabama, Howard University in Washington, D.C., Hampton Institute in Virginia, and the Coffey School of Aeronautics in Chicago.

By 1941, one hundred and two black pilots, a tenfold increase in just ten years, were flying. Also that year, the United States Army Air Corps activated the 99th Fighter Squadron, but, because of race, the squadron was considered a separate black air force.

Despite continuing segregation, the African-American role in aviation had begun to change. In the face of opposition by the Army Air Corps, Congress enacted legislation to activate the all-black 99th Fighter Squadron that reached the North African combat zone in 1943. Three additional black air units, the 100th, the

301st, and 302nd Fighter Squadrons, joined them and formed the 332nd Fighter Group. They fought in Allied campaigns in North Africa, Sicily, and Italy. Known as the Red Tails, the group was successful in battle. Men like Charles Hall, who was the first black pilot to down an enemy aircraft, and Andrew Turner, who flew sixty-nine successful missions, received the Distinguished Flying Cross and carried the dreams of Bessie Coleman, William Powell, James Banning, and Hubert Julian to new heights.

Those black pilots had been right. Equality in the sky had led to equality on the ground. They risked their lives and fortunes and faced ridicule and untold humiliation to emerge triumphant.

❋ ❋ ❋

My dad said that when you were up there in the sky, you could see everything. Everything that looked so big on the ground looked so small in the air, and you were above it all. For just a little while you were closer to where God was, and you felt the power and excitement that came from being one of the few who could do that.

David Lloyd George, former prime minister of England, said, "They were the intrepid Birdmen. Mounting frail wings and taking off into a wind-driven sky. They were the cavalry of the clouds. They were the knights of the air."

And for just a little while, my dad was too.

Girls

Growing up is hard. And growing up on the eve of the twenty-first century must be the toughest thing imaginable. So many temptations, challenges, expectations, and responsibilities exist for young people, especially boys, and especially when it comes to boy and girl interactions. Knowing what to say, when to say it, how to say it, and who to say it to when you're trying to impress someone is difficult. Here's my story of trying to deal with puberty, girls, and hormones.

* * *

When I was in the sixth grade, I began an odyssey into uncharted territory. This odyssey I could not control and I had no power to stop. From the time I woke up in the morning until I went to bed at night, my mind was absorbed by this subject.

When I played baseball, it was there. When I ran for a touchdown, it was there. Helping my dad in the garden, eating dinner, walking to the store for my mom, even at church on Sunday mornings, I could not stop thinking about it.

I had discovered girls.

They were all I thought about. It was as if I were under a spell, powerless to control my own thoughts.

All of a sudden, girls began looking good to me. Every bump, every curve, every strand of hair, every gesture, every smile.

I had never noticed them that much before, but now girls

were OK! They had always been there, but for some reason they didn't register in my brain until the sixth grade. When I was younger, I guess I had had too many other things to do. I had to play baseball during the summer, football in the fall, and basketball during the winter months. I had to help my dad cut the grass, change the oil, bleed the brakes, and repack the wheelbearings on his truck. Why, I even had to go to work with him during the summer and learn to lay bricks in order to earn a little extra money. So I was busy. When I wasn't helping him do something out in the yard, I was washing dishes, cleaning my room, or playing with my sister and brother.

Of course, my sister was a girl, sort of, but that was not the same. There was nothing about her that made me think of girls either way. She was just my sister.

But when I reached the sixth grade, everything started changing. I started growing. Man, was I growing, and I started noticing things about myself and my other friends that I hadn't noticed before. I mean, I was growing hairs under my arms!

Even the girls who lived in my neighborhood—the ones who were so stuck-up and always teasing me about my weight—started changing. Their hair, their legs, the way they smelled, talked, and acted were different.

For instance, Sharon Jones lived four houses down from me. We played together, especially when I couldn't find any of the boys to play basketball. She'd come over and we'd play basketball together.

But now, when she came over, I could hardly concentrate on the game. When she went up for a jump shot or jumped up for a rebound, I couldn't take my eyes off of her. My habit was to try to get the rebound and go for two points myself, but instead I found myself standing back watching her jump. There was something about the way she bounced that got my attention.

When I checked her, I didn't normally worry about whether I was too close or whether I'd hurt her or not. Now every time I checked her, I was careful not to bump into her.

She noticed my behavior, too, because whenever I was noticing, you know, these things, she'd say, "What are you looking at? Are you going to play or what?"

I was in a daze around girls. I couldn't help myself. I'd be eating dinner, and a girl would pop up in my mind. I'd be drying dishes, and I'd see Pamela Brown's face. I'd be walking to the store for Mama to get the usual—a loaf of bread, a pack of cigarettes (Marlboro with the fliptop box), a Dream Sickle, a Brown Mule, and some Bazooka Joe bubble gum for me—but instead of thinking about whether I had enough to buy a pack of Wise Potato Chips, I'd be thinking about Donna Armstead.

And if I saw a girl at the store, I was just a basket case. I'd come back home with two Hostess Twinkies, no cigarettes, no bread, and I'd be walking up my driveway before I even realized it.

I had it bad.

Rufus, my best friend, always had answers for these kinds of things, so I asked him about it. He said it was nothing to worry about, that it was happening to him, too. In fact, he said that he had been calling a girl we both knew from school and talking to her on the phone.

I thought that was the bravest thing. But that's how he was—brave. Not only was he one of the smartest boys in the sixth grade, he also had a style about him. He always seemed to be in control. He always knew the right thing to say to the teacher. He always read the best in class. He always won the Friday spelling bee. But I didn't mind that. He was my best friend, and his success was my success.

He always included me in everything he did. We went bird hunting together with our BB guns, we climbed trees together, and we took walks in the woods.

Our favorite game to play was Swing Down. We had a special tree, not really very big, and we'd climb to the top. The closer you got to the top of the tree where the branches narrowed, the more dangerous it became. We'd climb to the top, grabbing the tree by its branches, and swing down to the ground. We climbed that tree so much, it had started to bend.

We also had a special place by a creek near where we lived. We'd sit there and talk about everything from girls to our parents while we watched salamanders dart back and forth through the leaves and the water. I'd tell him a lie about kissing Cynthia Weeks, and he'd tell me one about smooching with Barbara Dandridge.

We even tried our first cigar together. We were behind my dad's smokehouse. I had gotten one of my dad's Roi Tan cigars from the big box they came in.

Daddy wasn't much of a smoker, and he smoked cigars only when we had company. I always figured he did it to show off, not because he was serious about smoking. Anyway, I figured he wouldn't miss one cigar.

Rufus brought the box of matches. I pulled the wrapper off the cigar, licked if from tip to stump as I had seen Daddy do, and left the paper gold ring on it, just as Daddy did. I asked Rufus to light me up. I took five big draws off of the cigar before it was lit properly.

By the time I had inhaled five breaths of that cigar, I was ready to pass it to Rufus! I was coughing and feeling pretty woozy, but I didn't want Rufus to know, so I said, "Smooth!" I think he knew I was lying, but he took his turn anyway.

He took six big drags from it. He had to outdo me, of course. He started coughing, too. All of a sudden, his face began to change color. Rufus was very dark-skinned, but when he took those draws, I swear his face turned yellow. He doubled over, dropped the cigar to the ground, mumbled something about his stomach, and started home. He didn't straighten up until he got to his back door. We never told anyone about that day, and we never smoked a cigar again either.

In spite of that experience, Rufus was usually the leader in all things, so it was no surprise to me that he'd taken the first step in the girl arena.

I listened to him talk on the phone, and it was like watching a master. He was so cool. His voice was husky and low, barely above a whisper. He'd prop himself into a corner and he'd play with the phone cord as he talked.

Most of the time they'd talk about school or about other girls or boys they both knew. Sometimes the girl would talk about her brother, and he'd talk about his little sister.

As I watched him in action, though, it didn't seem too difficult, so one day we experimented. He told the girl I was there and that he was going to put me on the phone.

I panicked! I motioned to him not to do it, but it was too late. He was handing me the phone.

I took it and said, "Hello?" That's all I remember. I don't know to this day what she said or what I said. I remember thinking her voice was so soft and gentle. But I was so nervous I could hardly hold the phone.

I knew I must have sounded like a turkey. After all, she had been talking to the king; she had been talking to Rufus. I'd definitely sound like a jerk compared to him. He finally took the phone from me, and I went home, embarrassed and disappointed in myself.

I didn't want to go in the house, so I went out in the yard to shoot some baskets. I started playing a game of Around the World. That was my best game. I could circle the basketball rack and hit every shot.

I'd been playing by myself for about fifteen minutes when Sharon, who was taking out the trash, saw me. She dropped the trash can and came bounding over to join me.

You can guess what happened. From the time I saw her coming, I missed every shot. My heart began to pound, and I lost all concentration.

Finally, I slammed the ball down and cursed.

"What's the matter?" she asked as she picked up the basketball to take a shot.

"Nothing!" I answered eloquently.

"You been acting crazy for some time now, Rex. It's like you're in a daze sometimes. What's wrong with you?"

"I don't want to talk about it, Sharon. You'll just think I'm stupid anyway," I said, rebounding the ball and flubbing another shot.

"How do you know what I'll think before you even say anything?"

"I just know, that's all," I said.

"If I didn't care about you, I wouldn't even ask. You just can't talk to anyone except Rufus Harewood. You think the sun rises and sets on him," she said accusingly.

"He's my best friend," I said. "He's a good guy and he looks out for me and stuff." Another eloquent statement. "Rufus is real smart, and he knows how to talk to grown-ups, and he can play basketball like nobody's business and he's ... he's cool. I don't even know why he hangs out with me. I can't do anything right. The girls all think I'm stupid, and the boys think that if it weren't for Rufus, I wouldn't have any friends at all. Plus there's this ... I don't know ... I'm thinking about stuff I've never thought about before."

"Stuff like what?" she asked.

"I don't want to talk anymore," I said. "I've already said too much. You probably think I'm stupid now."

"Rex, you are not stupid, and most girls I know don't think so either. Most of them think you're kinda cute."

"They do?" I said, surprised.

"Yes. Most of them wonder why you spend so much time around Rufus. One of them was even going to send you a note in class the other day, but you started talking to Rufus so she didn't send it."

"Who was it?" I asked, with my eyes bulging.

"That's for me to know and for you to find out. But I will tell you this: I think you hang around Rufus too much. If you were by yourself sometimes, you'd be surprised at how many girls might talk to you. When you're not around, they're always asking me what you're really like."

I wanted to ask her what she said to them, but I was too scared to ask and too afraid that her answer would make me feel worse.

"Know what I told them?" she asked, anticipating my thoughts.

"Yeah," I said. But I wanted to add: Only if it's good.

"I told them you're a different person. More confident and more fun to be around, especially when you aren't thinking so much. That's your problem," she said, taking a shot at the basket. "You think too much. Sometimes I can see your eyes just darting back and forth because so much is happening in your head."

"You can see that?" I asked.

"Sure I can. I can tell when you're angry, sad, frustrated, and even happy. But that doesn't happen very often.

"You've got to stop being so serious and just have some fun. And try doing it without Rufus. You should stop worrying about what people will think and just be honest about the way you feel."

"Yeah, you say that, but most girls just want boys who talk

smooth, and play on the junior varsity squad, and dress and act cool. Rufus is the most popular boy in sixth grade, and it's because he does all those things."

"A girl might like that for a little while but not for long. And any girl that thinks like that is probably not worth the trouble."

Man, I thought to myself, Sharon is smarter than I thought she was. Maybe I should do as she says. It can't hurt to try.

Just then she picked up the basketball, threw it to me, and said, "Take a shot." I did, and I hit it!

"Hot dog!" I said excitedly. I then threw it to her and said, "You take one."

She took her shot, and I looked at her as she bounced. I smiled broadly. She noticed me and said, as she usually did, "What are you looking at? Are you going to play basketball or what?"

"You," I said. "I'm looking at you, because you look good to me."

She turned beet red, threw the ball at me, smiled, and said, "See what I mean? You've wanted to say that for a long time, haven't you? You're not bad looking yourself."

I threw the ball back to her, and she made two points. Yep, I thought, Sharon's OK. Maybe I'll call her tonight.

I got the ball, shot again, and *swish*. Two more points.

Going to the Drive-in Movies

My fifteen-year-old son is entering a time that, for him, is exciting and new—that time when he discovers girls and begins to think of them as something other than pests or nuisances. As I watch him going through the rituals of flirting and the excitement of discovering himself and deciding what and who he wants to be, I naturally think about myself when I was his age, when tennis shoes did not cost one hundred dollars and a Starter jacket had yet to be created.

In my day—the 1960s—young men who were too young to go to clubs and too old to just sit at home had few places to take their dates. You could go and visit them at their homes and hope their little sisters and brothers weren't too obnoxious. You could take them to church and make points with their parents, but even that got boring after a while.

Sure, dances were held in the local elementary school's cafeteria and at the local community center or Elks Hall and Christmas Holly Balls and Halloween and Valentine's Day parties.

And there were fast food places like Riches, What-A-Burger, and McDonald's, but they weren't as popular as they are today, and none of them had drive-through windows. The burgers were too flat, the bread too thin, and I always hated the onions and sesame seed buns at McDonald's. You couldn't have it your way back then—what you got was what you got.

But as I grew older and got a driver's license, the one place I remember most of all was the drive-in movies, a hangout that could be found in every neighborhood. Today, they are mostly a relic of the past.

The drive-in was neat, because it provided a chance to be private in a public place—a public lover's lane where no one looked at you strangely if you kissed a girl. And it was much better than watching television at home or even going to a sit-down movie theater, because if you wanted to talk with your date, you could. No one would tell you to hush. If you wanted to bring popcorn from home, you could. If you wanted to listen to music while you waited for the movie to start, instead of watching advertisements for tasteless food, you could. If it was winter, you could turn on the car engine and get warm, or, even better, you could bring a blanket and snuggle. If it was summer, in the South at least, you always had to worry about mosquitoes. But even a few bites was a small price to pay for the chance to take out your best girl and spend some time alone together.

* * *

I don't think my adolescent years would have been half as pleasant if it hadn't been for drive-in movies. Girls and drive-in movies went together like grilled cheese and bread. And though I had gone to drive-in movies as a child, going there with girls was an entirely new experience. With girls my life changed drastically.

Before I became a teenager, I didn't worry about many things. I worried mostly about playing sports and getting to school on time. My favorite times were summer vacations, holidays, snow days, and visits to my grandparents in the country.

But girls added stress to my life and made me consider things that I had never thought of before: How do I find out if a girl really likes me? How do I say something to her that doesn't sound dumb? What can I do to get her to notice me? Does she think I'm cute? Does she like chunky guys? Will she ever kiss me?

Is my cologne too strong? Did I put on deodorant this morning? Does my breath smell? After girls entered my consciousness, my mind swirled with these kinds of never-ending dilemmas and fears.

I cannot count how many Banlon shirts I bought with particular girls in mind, or how much Royal Crown hair grease I put on my hair so that it lay just right. I even put a stocking cap on my head before I went to bed at night to create waves in my hair. I wish I had a dime for the number of times I splashed on Hai Karate cologne before a date.

From Tom McCann's I bought all my gray Hush Puppies, white bucks, and those shoes that had no shoelaces that are fastened shut by pushing the tongue down. I spent more money on clothes at Fine's Men's Shops and Arthur's than most teenagers today spend at Hecht's and J.C. Penney. And you could not tell me I wasn't cool with my Chuck Taylor Converse All Stars, the most popular tennis shoes among black boys in the 1960s and 1970s. I didn't even know who Chuck Taylor was, but if you didn't have those tennis shoes in my neighborhood, you definitely were not a member of the in-crowd, and P.F. Flyers, a less expensive tennis shoe, were not an adequate substitute!

The creases in my dress pants always had to be just right. Ironing wouldn't do; I took those pants to the cleaners. No jeans—they were for farmers. And my hair—I'd put Ultra Sheen, Vaseline Hair Tonic, Royal Crown, or Posner Bergamot on it. My mama was a beautician, and she used Posner Bergamot to fix hair. When she wasn't looking, I'd sneak a little for myself.

To top off the outfit, I had to have a good-looking top piece, preferably wide-brimmed, that cocked to one side, that I could hide behind. We chose hats that made us look mysterious, aloof, self-assured, and in control. We called that cool.

After a quick check in the mirror to make sure the ensemble's colors were matching, I was ready to go. But before going on a date to the drive-in, you had to have one—a date that is.

Getting a date was easily the most humiliating experience of my young life. I was simply awful at asking a girl out on a date. Guys had to do all the work. Girls just waited for the phone to ring. We had to ask. We had to be the ones to go through the humiliation. And if you didn't do it right, they'd say no, and let me tell you, no matter how cool you thought you were, no was major rejection. It was proof positive that you had not mastered the art of rapping. In those days, rapping just meant someone wasn't a convincing talker and was not very good at the art of persuasion.

Rejection was especially hard for me. It was proof positive that I was the dumbest person on my street, that I was too fat and girls didn't like me, that Daddy should have signed the permission slip to let me play football. After all, the athletes got all the girls. Rejection signaled that my life was ruined, and I was doomed to spend the rest of my days living in the woods and foraging for roots and berries as hermits did.

I must admit that other boys handled rejection much better than I did. They tried to play it off by saying something like, "Ha, ha, I was just kidding. You know I'm not that desperate," or "You just passed up a good thing, girl," or "You'd better go find yourself somebody outside our neighborhood since you so choosy!" I could never think of witty comebacks like that. I didn't even try to dismiss it. Each girl who rejected me knew she had broken my heart and my spirit.

Kenneth, my best friend at the time, said I needed to work on my rap, so I went through two weeks of training with him. We called it Phone Rap 101. He taught me how to sing, and we'd listen to local deejays as they rapped on the radio:

Hot dog, hot dog, please don't go.
Don't you worry, baby, I won't stray until the sands
of time have passed away.

I was flabbergasted. I said, "Kenneth, girls fall for that?"
He answered, "Every time."

Well, it worked, because I got a date two weeks later. I knew I had her when I heard her sigh after I sang, "Baby, I'm Yours."

Now that I had a date and looked good, I had to have some wheels. Certainly not my own, but I had to make my parents' car, actually my mom's car, look as snazzy as possible.

We had a ten-year-old, 1959 black Plymouth Savoy that I could make shine like new money. The fabric overhead had torn at a right angle in the middle of the ceiling, and the edge dangled down on top of my hair and draped in the middle of the front seat. Grease stains spotted the fabric in every spot where it had rubbed against my Ultra-Sheened afro. I taped it up, but just about the time my date got in the car, it always came loose. I used to convince myself that since the outside of the car looked good, the girls would simply ignore the upholstery.

My dates were usually from my neighborhood. It was tricky dating girls from my own neighborhood. I went to church and school with them. I knew their parents, and their parents knew me. I had to be on my best behavior because one wrong move would mean a first date would be the last. I had to be cool. A man's reputation was his most prized possession.

Now, I never dated a girl who wasn't hungry, and they never brought any money of their own. I don't know how other guys fared, but all of my dates were paupers. They never even offered to pay for a meal. I guess they felt free food was their payment for going out with me and having to deal with my weak attempts to kiss and grope them all night. So we all had to have either well-to-do parents or a part-time job. Most of the people I knew had part-time jobs, which basically paid for three things—clothes, food, and gas.

The drive-in movie in Yorktown, Virginia, sat out in a big field that had been divided into rows of long hills. When cars pulled up to face the huge outdoor movie screen, they parked on an incline facing the screen. This way, the viewer's line of vision was at the same angle as the screen. Each row had about fifteen or twenty metal poles stuck in the ground with detachable speakers coming out of each side for two cars. Each speaker had two feet of cord and a large protruding extension on the opposite side that looked like a capital "H" with the top part of the "H" cut off. You simply rolled down the window, hooked the speaker to the window, and adjusted the volume.

We paid about two dollars and could watch movies until around midnight, which was when the girls had to be home anyway.

All drive-ins had little huts in the middle of the field that housed the projection room, bathrooms, and snack stand with hot dogs, hamburgers, barbecue, and, of course, fried chicken that was so tough it was like trying to eat strips of rubber.

The best part was when I got to smooch with the girl. You had to be careful though. There couldn't be too much smooching because there were people who worked for the drive-in and did nothing but walk by and shine flashlights in cars. You did not want to be caught in a compromising position. You might as well kiss dating goodbye if you let that happen. You always protected a girl's honor—if you wanted to go out with her again.

So smooching was another skill I had to master with little or no practice. And a skill it was. A boy never tried anything until he fed his date. He never rushed into anything no matter how turned on he was or how good she looked and smelled. He never stared at certain parts of her body no matter how much they protruded or how short her dress was. He had to balance his tension and stress with her tolerance level. He did not want to make her angry or have her think that all he had on his mind was sex. After all, he thought more of her than that.

Time, however, was also a factor. Once the final feature started, a guy knew he didn't have much time to make his move. So the strategy had to be tight, the movements smooth and innocent. The worst thing that could happen on a date was to have them run the second feature and have your date get interested in it. That was the death knell of any smooching. You might as well hang it up.

But one night I had a date who was very special. It was our third date, and everything meshed just right. She was beautiful. There had been something special about her from the beginning, but I just couldn't put my finger on what it was. After we had eaten and our food had had time to digest, I moved maybe a half cheek closer to her. She responded by moving closer to me. After a particularly funny part in the movie, I laughed and moved my head closer to hers. When I did that, she looked at me and smiled. Our eyes met. Ever so gently I moved closer to her and we kissed.

I don't remember the rest of the movie, because we began talking, and in between the talking, we'd hold hands and kiss.

It was one of the best times I can remember. The smooching was good, but she was fun to be with as well. She seemed interested in the same kinds of things I was and truly cared about what I had to say. As the movie ended and the credits rolled, I reached over to kiss her once more. Just then the torn cloth from the car ceiling dropped down into our faces, blocking our lips. She reached up, moved the cloth out of the way, and said, "You know, my dad owns an auto body shop. Maybe he can fix this for you." Then she kissed me.

When the screen went dark, I started the car and pulled out of the drive-in. I drove as slowly as I could. I wanted the moment to last as long as possible.

We finally arrived at her house, and I walked her to the front door. We kissed one last time. As I got into my car and pulled away, I remember thinking that she was special.

After twenty-three years of marriage, I can tell you. . . I was right. Drive-in movies—I miss them.

Additional Resources

I can only hope that this book has created a curiosity about the African-American experience. Below are some of the books I used to help me write this book. By no means is this a complete list of books about African Americans. It serves only as a beginning. Enjoy the journey.

Asante, Molefi K. *The Historical and Cultural Atlas of African Americans*. New York: MacMillan Publishing Company, 1981.

Botkin, B.A., ed. *Lay My Burden Down: A Folk History of Slavery*. Original Material. Federal Works Project of the Works Progress Administration, 1939. Chicago: University of Chicago Press, 1977.

Bush, Barbara. *Slave Women in Caribbean Society, 1650-1838*. Bloomington: Indiana University Press, 1990.

Cameron, James. *A Time of Terror*. Milwaukee: TD Publications, 1982.

Conway, Cee Cee B. *African Banjo Echoes in Appalachia: A Study of Folk Traditions*. Knoxville: University of Tennessee Press, 1995.

Epstein, Dena. *Sinful Tunes and Spirituals: Black Folk Music to the Civil War*. Chicago: University of Illinois Press, 1977.

Everett, Susanne. *History of Slavery*. Secaucus: Chartwell Books, 1993.

Hardesty, Von, and Dominick Pisano. *Black Wings: The American Black in Aviation*. Washington, D.C.: National Air and Space Museum, Smithsonian Institution, 1983.

Horton, James Oliver. *Free People of Color: Inside the African American Community*. Washington: Smithsonian Institution Press, 1993.

Isaacs, Rhys. *The Transformation of Virginia, 1740-1790: Community, Religion, and Authority*. Chapel Hill: University of North Carolina Press, 1982.

Katz, William Loren. *Eyewitness: The Negro in American History*. New York: Pitman Publishing Corporation, 1971.

McDaniel, George. *Hearth and Home: Preserving a Peoples Culture*. Philadelphia: Temple University Press, 1981.

Northup, Solomon. *Twelve Years a Slave*. Baton Rouge: Louisiana State University Press, 1983.

Nugent, John Peer. *The Black Eagle*. New York: Stein and Day, 1971.

Raboteau, Albert J. *Slave Religion: The "Invisible Institution" in the Antebellum South*. New York: Oxford University Press, 1978.

Rawley, James. *The Transatlantic Slave Trade: A History*. New York: Norton, 1981.

Rich, Doris L. *Queen Bess: Daredevil Aviator*. Washington, D.C.: Smithsonian Institution Press, 1993.

Southern, Eileen. *The Music of Black Americans*. New York: Norton, 1971.

Takaki, Ronald. *A Different Mirror: The Making of Multicultural America*. Boston: Little, Brown, & Co., 1993.